Day by Day in God's Kingdom

A Discipleship Journal

Avery T. Willis, Jr.
& J. David Carter

Foreword by Henry T. Blackaby

LifeWay Press
Nashville, Tennessee

ISBN 0-7673-2577-X

Dewey Decimal Classification: 242.2
Subject Heading: DISCIPLESHIP

Printed in the United States of America

LifeWay Press
127 Ninth Avenue, North
Nashville, Tennessee 37234

Contents

Foreword

When God speaks, it is crucial to write down what He says! Through Moses, God taught the Israelites that "man does not live on bread alone but on every word that comes from the mouth of the Lord" (Deut. 8:3). Later in Deuteronomy 32:47 Moses reminded them that when God spoke, His words were " 'not just idle words for you—they are your life.' " Therefore, the most significant moments in any person's life are his or her encounters with God when He speaks. These encounters come as you study God's Word and the Spirit of God teaches you and guides you into all truth (see John 14:25-26; 16:12-14). He also speaks when you pray; He speaks in your marketplace; and He speaks in a completely different way as you live your Christian life in the midst of God's people, your church.

What a joy, an honor, and a responsibility it is to journal, or record, your encounters with God. I have done this for years. Writing down what God says in my quiet time benefits me in several ways.

- Journaling *helps me clarify* what I have received from God. The act of writing what God has revealed lets me concentrate on what He has said and lets me be sure I have recorded it exactly as He said it.

- Journaling *helps me make commitments* to God by recording specific responses. Every encounter with God requires a response. I am never the same again when God speaks. As His servant I seek to respond in immediate obedience. And I make a commitment to follow through in that obedience. Writing it down helps me follow through with that response to God.

- Journaling *helps me remember* my commitments made sincerely in God's presence. Before I began to record my encounters with God, I would forget most of what I had experienced within a few days. By reading my journal, however, I can remember my commitment and continue to be obedient.

- Journaling *helps me recall* these special moments so that I can be a more faithful servant of God. Immediate review keeps fresh my day-by-day relationship with God. The moment God speaks to me is a moment I want to treasure. Writing it down seals that moment in my life.

- Journaling *gives me a bigger picture* of God's activity in my life and around my life. God moves progressively. He often waits for my obedience before committing to me His next step. The longer I walk with God and keep a record of that relationship, the more clearly I see what God is doing. It is like reading the Old Testament and then discovering in the New Testament all that God had been doing over the centuries. Often, the bigger picture gives me meaning and security for the future because I can see what He is doing. As I review weekly or monthly, I can see a pattern or a progression in God's activity. Certain journal entries become spiritual markers, giving me a clear direction for my life.

This journal can be one of your most useful resources in your walk with God because it will help you be faithful in spending time with God. It also provides an easily accessible place to write your commitments in prayer. God will regularly bring to your awareness someone for whom He wants you to pray. Record the name on one of the prayer lists at the back of this journal and continue praying until God has brought about His purposes for that person's life. This journal has other wonderful extras to help you stay focused on an intimate walk with God. Use it faithfully and carefully as a good steward of God's grace.

Writing down your experiences with God will change your life and will be pleasing to God.

HENRY T. BLACKABY

How to use Your Discipleship Journal

Believers' relationships with God are strengthened when we spend time committed only to Him. During our regular times with God, He provides the guidance we need to live victorious Christian lives.

Day by Day in God's Kingdom is a journal you can use during your daily quiet time to keep records of your communication with God. It provides 13 weeks of daily activities designed to help you understand and practice six essential Christian disciplines. It suggests focal Scripture passages for study during your daily quiet time and for weekly memorization. You will also read a weekly introduction that explains and illustrates one of the six disciplines you are learning to incorporate into your life.

Essential Christian Disciplines

Growing Christians live disciplined Christian lives. Christian disciplines are spiritual activities practiced by persons who want to stay fit in their personal, family, professional, and public lives. As you spend time with God each day, this discipleship journal guides you to develop the following six Christian disciplines. Practicing these disciplines will lead you to a deeper relationship with God and to a life of obedient service to Him.

Spend time with the Master. Growing disciples read their Bibles and pray every day. The best time is the first thing in the morning, but the important point is to find a time that best fits your lifestyle and commit to keep an appointment with God at this time every day. During this time keep a record of what God says to you and of what you say to God.

Live in the Word. The Word is both the living Word, Jesus Christ, and the written Word, the Bible. As you read the Bible, God speaks to you. Growing disciples need to hear what God says through His Word.

Pray in faith. Prayer is an integral part of a believer's walk with the Lord. Personal prayer, in which you talk and listen to God, supports a Christian lifestyle. Believers depend on one another for prayer support for the smallest to the largest matters in life. Growing disciples minister to others through prayer.

Fellowship with believers. Christians need one another. You grow by being part of the body of Christ, in which each person benefits from the spiritual gifts of others. Genuine Christian fellowship includes a commitment to love those who share faith in Jesus Christ. Fellowship provides support, leadership, accountability, strength, encouragement, and direction for a unified mission.

Witness to the world. Witnessing is bearing spiritual fruit that identifies you as someone who walks with Jesus Christ. Witnessing is living in a manner that bears evidence of a strength that comes only from the Lord and that draws others to Christ. Witnessing is also sharing the good news of Jesus Christ. Growing disciples also have the right and responsibility to present the gospel to others.

Minister to others. Like the Good Samaritan (see Luke 10:25-37), growing disciples minister unselfishly, even to persons who have nothing to give in return. You minister because you walk in a relationship with Christ, who touched the untouchable; who went home with persons rejected by society; and who, while physically tired, taught the crowds and miraculously fed them. Ministry gives beyond what is required or expected.

Prayer Guidance

Your daily prayer times will extend beyond prayer for immediate concerns. Ongoing prayer lists are provided at the back of your journal for daily, weekly, and monthly prayer concerns (pp. 178–79). Either your daily "Pray in Faith" activity will suggest which list to use for a particular request, or you can choose the list for each prayer request. You may move your requests from one list to another as you wish, and you may photocopy the lists as needed. Each time you add a request, you assume additional responsibility to pray. If maintaining prayer lists is new to you, begin where you are and develop your lists as your prayer ministry grows. Additional instructions for using your prayer lists may be found on page 177.

Guidance for identifying spiritual markers is provided on page 177, and a chart for recording spiritual markers appears on page 180. Reserve this section for times when God breaks through with a special experience that becomes a big event in your life. For example, the Israelites referred to the crossing of the Red Sea as an event God used to teach them to depend on Him. These special times increase our knowledge of God and our faith. A spiritual marker is a faith builder.

Guidance is provided on pages 153–54 for an extended time with God during or after week 13, in which you can evaluate your spiritual growth during the weeks you have kept this journal.

Devotional Uses

Day by Day in God's Kingdom is designed for you to use with your Bible as you study the suggested Scripture references. However, if you are using other devotional material such as a magazine or book during your quiet time or if you are studying a discipleship course, you can still use this journal to keep a daily record of God's activity in your life. Simply substitute the Scriptures suggested in the other material for the ones provided in *Day by Day in God's Kingdom*. You will find that the activities in this journal apply to any Scriptures you are studying.

Continuing to Grow

Because *Day by Day in God's Kingdom* is a discipleship journal, the activities help you continue an ongoing process of spiritual growth. Therefore, the activities in this journal are not outdated with one use. They are designed for repeated use by a growing disciple. Your life is always changing, so your response to an activity today may be different from your response to the activity one year from now. When you finish this journal, order another copy to continue keeping records of what God is doing in your life. When you review your journal notes, you will discover ways God had prepared you for future situations. You can keep your journal like a diary to measure your spiritual growth and your progress toward your life goals.

Additional copies of *Day by Day in God's Kingdom* (item 0-7673-2577-X) may be purchased by contacting the Customer Service Center; 127 Ninth Avenue, North; Nashville, TN 37234; 1-800-458-2772; or by visiting a Baptist Book Store or a Lifeway Christian Store.

Developing Christian disciplines is the most important way you can spend your time as a disciple of Jesus Christ. As you make these disciplines an integral part of your life, you will experience a closer walk of faithful obedience to your Lord and Master.

WEEK 1

SPEND TIME WITH THE MASTER

†

AVERY T. WILLIS, JR.

"I am the vine; you are the branches. If a man remains in me and I in him, he will bear much fruit; apart from me you can do nothing,' " Jesus said in John 15:5. This verse tells you the secret of the Christian life from God's perspective. He loves you and wants to have fellowship with you. Discipleship is developing a personal, lifelong, obedient relationship with Jesus Christ. Your remaining in Him is of ultimate importance to God. His plans for you include your spending time with Him.

For a child, love is spelled T-I-M-E. God gave you 24 hours a day. As His child, what portion of the day do you think He wants to spend with you? All of it. He said, " 'Surely I am with you always, to the very end of the age' " (Matt. 28:20). He is with you every waking and sleeping hour. How much time do you want to spend with Him? It can be 24 hours a day. The psalmist said:

> How precious to me are your thoughts, O God!
>   How vast is the sum of them!
> Were I to count them,
>   they would outnumber the grains of sand.
> When I awake,
>   I am still with you (Ps. 139:17-18).

If you continually memorize and meditate on His Word, you will be assured of His presence even when you wake up.

Spending time with the Master is not a question of God's making time for you but of your making time for Him. Affirm the Lord's presence with your first waking thought each day.

To experience God's presence all day, begin the day with Him. The first priority of the day is to listen to God through His Word and to talk with Him through prayer. If you are to remain in Him throughout the day, you need to begin the day with Him.

Once a daily quiet time is established, begin working on constantly being led by the Spirit. Think of your Bible as a telephone. If you receive and meditate on Scripture daily, you will be aware of Him and His thoughts. He has constant access to you when you remain in His Word. You have constant access to Him by praying without ceasing. The best way to understand what it means to pray without ceasing is to picture a husband and wife or a couple of good friends riding through the countryside together on a trip. You do not have to talk constantly to enjoy each other's company. Even if others are along, you are aware of that special person's presence. Likewise, we spend time with God in a personal, intimate relationship. The secret is to spend time with the Master in a loving relationship each day.

As you read, study, memorize, and apply Scripture, God will talk to you. As you preview the upcoming day with Him, you can have conversations about what is most important to you and to Him. Begin establishing the priority of having a quiet time with God every morning by spending a few minutes with Him. As you grow in maturity, you will spend more and more time with the Father, just as Jesus did: "Very early in the morning, while it was still dark, Jesus got up, left the house and went off to a solitary place, where he prayed" (Mark 1:35).

Get in the habit of writing what God says to you and a summary of what you say to Him as you read your Bible each day. Your journal will become a living testimony to your relationship. Your life will bear fruit, and God will be glorified.

If you were told that the president of the United States would be at your house at 6:00 a.m. tomorrow, would you be ready? Of course. One much greater than the president is patiently waiting for you to meet with Him each morning and abide in Him throughout the day. Day by day as you work through this journal, read the Word, pray in faith, and obey His commands, you will discover the secret of His presence and will begin to see things as He sees them.

This Week's Suggested Scripture Readings

The following Scriptures support the discipline of spending time with the Master. Choose from these Scriptures to complete your "Live in the Word" assignment each day this week or substitute other Scriptures you have selected.

Day 1—Genesis 28:16-19; Luke 6:12
Day 2—Exodus 33:9-11; Luke 24:15,32
Day 3—1 Samuel 1:19-20; Acts 4:13
Day 4—1 Samuel 15:11; Acts 10:2
Day 5—Psalm 5:3; 1 Corinthians 1:9

This Week's Suggested Memory Verses

Memorize one of the following verses this week or another verse you have selected.

- Psalm 5:3
- 1 Corinthians 1:9

DAY 1

Spend Time with the Master

Describe what your private time with God means to you.

Live in the Word

Write the reference of your selected Scripture reading for today.

Write the passage in the form of a prayer.

Pray in Faith

Pray the verse you wrote as a prayer. After you pray the verse, complete the following sentence.

It is God's will that I—

Fellowship with Believers

Choose an activity from the list on pages 165–68 to complete this week. Begin writing plans for completing it.

Witness to the World

Choose an activity from the list on pages 169–72 to complete this week. Begin writing plans for completing it.

Minister to Others

Choose an activity from the list on pages 173–76 to complete this week. Begin writing plans for completing it.

DAY 2

Spend Time with the Master
Write the reference of your selected Scripture reading for today.

Write the passage in the form of a prayer.

Live in the Word
Pray the verse you wrote as a prayer. After you pray that verse, complete the following sentence.

It is God's will that I—

Pray in Faith
One type of prayer is confession. To confess is to agree with God—to see sin as hideous and destructive, just as God sees it. When you confess, you not only admit your guilt but also place yourself in the hands of the only One who can forgive. In repenting of your sin, you turn away from your sin and toward God.

Name an area of your life in which you need to agree with God. Make that agreement in a written prayer.

Fellowship with Believers

Record your progress in completing the activity you chose for this week.

Witness to the World

Record your progress in completing the activity you chose for this week.

Minister to Others

Record your progress in completing the activity you chose for this week.

DAY 3

SPEND TIME WITH THE MASTER

What would you say to a 16-year-old who asked you why you have a daily quiet time? Write your response below.

LIVE IN THE WORD

Write the reference of your selected Scripture reading for today.

Write the memory verse you selected to memorize this week. Describe the value of that verse for you.

PRAY IN FAITH

Use part of today's prayer time to pray for a friend who is struggling. Write your prayer concern below and add the person's name to your daily prayer list on page 178.

Fellowship with Believers

Record your progress in completing the activity you chose for this week.

Witness to the World

Record your progress in completing the activity you chose for this week.

Minister to Others

Record your progress in completing the activity you chose for this week.

DAY 4

Spend Time with the Master

What is the difference between your quiet time with God using this journal and a quiet ride down the highway while you talk and listen to God? Write your answer below.

Live in the Word

Write the reference of your selected Scripture reading for today.

Choose one Christlike trait the passage identifies that you need and want in your life. Explain why you need that trait and how you can develop it.

Pray in Faith

Intercessory prayer is a ministry. As you pray for persons, write their concerns below and add their names to one of the prayer lists on pages 178–79.

Fellowship with Believers

Record your progress in completing the activity you chose for this week.

Witness to the World

Record your progress in completing the activity you chose for this week.

Minister to Others

Record your progress in completing the activity you chose for this week.

DAY 5

Spend Time with the Master
Review your journal notes for this week and write a short summary of what you have experienced in your time with God.

Live in the Word
Write the reference of your selected Scripture reading for today.

Choose and record a thought for the day that the passage expresses.

Pray in Faith
Include your pastor in your prayers today. Write your prayer below and ask God to bless him. Add his name to one of your prayer lists (pp. 178–79) if you have not already done so.

Fellowship with Believers

Record your progress in completing the activity you chose for this week.

Witness to the World

Record your progress in completing the activity you chose for this week.

Minister to Others

Record your progress in completing the activity you chose for this week.

WEEK 2

LIVE IN THE WORD

AVERY T. WILLIS, JR.

Jesus' entire life revolved around God's Word. He intends for the Word to be at the center of your life. He stated it this way: " 'If you hold to my teaching, you are really my disciples. Then you will know the truth, and the truth will set you free' " (John 8:31-32).

Jesus is the living Word: "In the beginning was the Word, and the Word was with God, and the Word was God" (John 1:1). The written Word testifies to and perfectly reflects what God has said and who Jesus is.

Jesus' ministry was a fulfillment of the Word: " 'This is what I told you while I was still with you: Everything must be fulfilled that is written about me in the Law of Moses, the Prophets and the Psalms' " (Luke 24:44).

Jesus often cited Scriptures He was fulfilling. He claimed that everything He said and did came from the Father, especially His words: " 'The words I say to you are not just my own. Rather, it is the Father, living in me, who is doing his work' " (John 14:10).

Jesus reported in His prayer to the Father that He had given words from the Father to His disciples: " 'I gave them the words you gave me and they accepted them' " (John 17:8). Not only did they accept them, but they also did them: " 'They were yours; you gave them to me and they have obeyed your word' " (John 17:6).

Jesus linked the teaching and the practice of the Word to greatness in the Kingdom: " 'Anyone who breaks one of the least of these commandments and teaches others to do the same will be called least in the kingdom of heaven, but whoever practices and teaches these commands will be called great in the kingdom of heaven' " (Matt. 5:19).

It should be clear that the way to live in the Word is to receive it, accept it as God's Word, believe it, and obey it. This is the mark by which others know that you are His disciple. When you put the Word into practice, you present the strongest witness to Christ. In fact, when Jesus was being tried, He was asked about His disciples and His teaching. The disciples were the living repository of His teaching—exhibit A. No wonder Jesus said that obeying His teaching is the mark of His disciples.

Sadly, many Christians do not take the commands of God's Word as something to be literally applied to their lives. They want to pick and choose what they obey. They want to be the lords of what they do. They have not totally surrendered to do whatever God tells them to.

On the other hand, when a Christian takes God's Word seriously, a dynamic relationship results. Doing God's Word provides a powerful connection with God, making it possible for you to live in Him. God can entrust His Word to disciples who obey it.

Have you come to the point in your spiritual development that you have not only accepted God's Word as truth but have also committed yourself to practice whatever God tells you to do through it? Once you do, God has full access to you, and you have full access to God. Jesus promised: " 'Whoever has my commands and obeys them, he is the one who loves me. My Father will love him, and we will come to him and make our home with him. He who does not love me will not obey my teaching' " (John 14:21,23-24).

A disciple knows the Word and obeys the Word. To live in the Word, you must receive the Word into your life by every possible avenue: listening, reading, studying, memorizing, meditating on, and applying it. Then you prove it in actual experience.

Living in the Word is as simple as that. Though it is simple, it is not easy. To obey the Word, we must abide in Christ. He is the one who obeys the Father as He lives in us: "It is God who works in you to will and to act according to his good purpose" (Phil. 2:13). He gives us the desire and the ability to obey Him.

This Week's Suggested Scripture Readings

The following Scriptures support the discipline of living in the Word. Choose from these Scriptures to complete your "Live in the Word" assignment each day this week or substitute other Scriptures you have selected.

Day 1—Deuteronomy 4:2,10; Psalm 119:103-105; Matthew 5:18-19
Day 2—Joshua 1:8; Proverbs 6:23; Luke 11:28; Ephesians 6:17
Day 3—Job 23:12; Jeremiah 15:16; Romans 7:12,22; 1 Thessalonians 2:13
Day 4—Psalm 12:6; Jeremiah 23:29; 1 Corinthians 10:11; 2 Timothy 3:16-17
Day 5—Psalm 19:7-11; Matthew 22:29; 2 Peter 1:19-21

This Week's Suggested Memory Verses

Memorize one of the following verses this week or another verse you have selected.

- Psalm 119:105
- Proverbs 6:23
- John 20:31
- 2 Timothy 3:16-17

DAY 1

Spend Time with the Master

Use a calendar to identify a day when you can spend an extended time with God during or after week 13. You will need to reserve at least three hours.

____

Live in the Word

Write the reference of your selected Scripture reading for today.

____

A life verse is a Bible verse that means more to you than any other. If you do not have a life verse, be alert to identifying it when God leads you to one. If you have a life verse, write it below.

____

____

____

____

____

Pray in Faith

Review your prayer lists on pages 178–79. You may need to update them or add requests. Organize your prayer times so that you pray from daily, weekly, and monthly prayer lists. Write two requests below to pray for today and describe the prayer concerns.

____

____

____

____

____

Fellowship with Believers

Choose an activity from the list on pages 165–68 to complete this week. Begin writing plans for completing it.

Witness to the World

Choose an activity from the list on pages 169–72 to complete this week. Begin writing plans for completing it.

Minister to Others

Choose an activity from the list on pages 173–76 to complete this week. Begin writing plans for completing it.

DAY 2

Spend Time with the Master

Spending time with the Master includes both Bible reading and prayer. On a scale of 1 to 10, with 10 being the highest value, write an *X* over the level of importance you gave a quiet time three months ago. Circle its present value to you.

1 2 3 4 5 6 7 8 9 10

Explain why you assigned the values you chose.

____

____

Live in the Word

Write the reference of your selected Scripture reading for today.

____

Record a new thought your Bible passage introduced to you.

____

____

____

Pray in Faith

Are you noticing the need to spend a larger part of your quiet time in prayer? ❑ Yes ❑ No Is it time for a stronger commitment to this private time? ❑ Yes ❑ No Before you make further commitments, ask God to lead you in this process. Write your prayer below.

____

____

____

____

Fellowship with Believers

Record your progress in completing the activity you chose for this week.

Witness to the World

Record your progress in completing the activity you chose for this week.

Minister to Others

Record your progress in completing the activity you chose for this week.

DAY 3

Spend Time with the Master

Write one thing you need to say to God during today's quiet time.

Live in the Word

Write the reference of your selected Scripture reading for today.

As you read your Bible passage, answer the question, *Do I listen to hear a word from God as I read?* ❑ Yes ❑ No Write what God said to you today.

Pray in Faith

Write at least one thing you need to say to God. Mention something you normally avoid talking to Him about. Pray it aloud to God.

Fellowship with Believers

Record your progress in completing the activity you chose for this week.

Witness to the World

Record your progress in completing the activity you chose for this week.

Minister to Others

Record your progress in completing the activity you chose for this week.

DAY 4

Spend Time with the Master

Recall one occurrence yesterday that you could have handled better if you had first consulted God about it. Explain why.

____

____

Live in the Word

Write the reference of your selected Scripture reading for today.

____

Yesterday you asked the question, *Do I listen to hear a word from God as I read?* Again write what God says to you through today's Bible passage.

____

____

____

____

Pray in Faith

One type of prayer is thanksgiving. Thanksgiving emerges from a deep sense of gratitude not only for material possessions but also for blessings that can be provided only by God: family, friends, salvation, God's grace and faithfulness, a part in God's kingdom, joy in Christ, and strength to serve Him, for example. Prayers of thanksgiving remind us of our dependence on the Lord.

Thank God for times when He warns you. Write your prayer below. Then say to God, Please show me when I stray and take the wrong path.

____

____

____

Fellowship with Believers
Record your progress in completing the activity you chose for this week.

Witness to the World
Record your progress in completing the activity you chose for this week.

Minister to Others
Record your progress in completing the activity you chose for this week.

DAY 5

Spend Time with the Master

Write the amount of time you plan to spend in your next quiet time.

____

What do you think that decision says about your commitment to spend time with your Master?

____

____

Live in the Word

Write the reference of your selected Scripture reading for today.

____

Write the name of someone with whom you can share this biblical thought today.

____

How do you feel that this person can benefit from this passage?

____

____

____

Pray in Faith

Choose a key thought in your Bible passage and write it as a prayer.

____

____

____

____

Fellowship with Believers

Record your progress in completing the activity you chose for this week.

Witness to the World

Record your progress in completing the activity you chose for this week.

Minister to Others

Record your progress in completing the activity you chose for this week.

WEEK 3

PRAY IN FAITH

J. DAVID CARTER

Jesus said, " 'Have faith in God' " (Mark 11:22). Faith rests in God. We do not have to develop faith to get things done. Our faith is not in things but in the Lord Jesus Christ. We are to trust Him. The question is, *Do I believe God?* Faith is taking God at His word: "This is the confidence we have in approaching God: that if we ask anything according to his will, he hears us. And if we know that he hears us—whatever we ask—we know that we have what we asked of him" (1 John 5:14-15).

One reason faith is so difficult to experience is that our nature is sinful, having witnessed lies, disillusionment, and failed integrity. Our faith need not rest in our own nature when we have received Christ's nature.

Praying in faith begins with God's Word: "Faith comes from hearing the message, and the message is heard through the word of Christ" (Rom. 10:17). Faith is based on God's truth, on hearing the message. God communicates truth to us through the Bible. When God speaks with a message we understand, it is as if He places a light on a verse that illuminates a meaning that applies to our situation.

When we have such an experience, we are to take it to Jesus to be our Mediator. Our faith rests in our Mediator. John 17 tells us that Jesus prays on our behalf, bringing our needs before the Father: " 'I pray for them. I am not praying for the world, but for those you have given me, for they are yours' " (John 17:9). Jesus prays for us. When God reveals a truth to you, pray to Jesus and ask Him to tell you how it should apply to your life.

Next, wait for the Holy Spirit to make the application: " 'When he, the Spirit of truth, comes, he will guide you into all truth. He will not speak on his own; he will speak only what he hears, and he will tell you what is yet to come. He will bring glory to me by taking from what is mine and making it known to you' " (John 16:13-14). The Holy Spirit takes the truth given by the Father and applies it to our lives. The experience of faith, then, is the Holy Spirit's work of applying God's truth to our lives.

Review the process. As you read the Bible, you discover a truth. You start thinking about what it means to you. Then the truth broadens your understanding to see more than words. You pray to Jesus, who is Truth, and ask Him to reveal what you should believe. What you believe is your faith applied. Then the Holy Spirit directs you to apply the truth to your life. That which is applied to your life requires a response. The response may require a major or minor adjustment in your life. Faith is making that adjustment.

So praying in faith is an integral part of a believer's walk with the Lord. Prayer is a testimony about your belief and trust in God. Personal prayer supports your Christian lifestyle. Praying in faith helps you maintain God's will for your life. And it comes with a gift: "If we are children, then we are heirs—heirs of God and co-heirs with Christ" (Rom. 8:17). When Jesus died, He left His heirs this inheritance. You receive it because of your relationship with Jesus. It is your possession of faith. You can count on it. You can rest in it. No one can take it away. It is yours, and it comes wrapped in a package of faith.

This Week's Suggested Scripture Readings

The following Scriptures support the discipline of praying in faith. Choose from these Scriptures to complete your "Live in the Word" assignment each day this week or substitute other Scriptures you have selected.

Day 1—Psalm 5:2-3; Matthew 6:5-8; 1 Thessalonians 5:17-18
Day 2—Psalm 8:1; Mark 11:24; 1 Timothy 2:8
Day 3—2 Chronicles 7:14; Psalm 13; Romans 12:12
Day 4—Psalm 55:16-17; Matthew 6:9-15; Matthew 8:8,10,13
Day 5—Psalm 141:1-2; Matthew 17:20; John 14:13-14

This Week's Suggested Memory Verses

Memorize one of the following verses this week or another verse you have selected.

- Psalm 8:1
- Mark 11:24
- Romans 12:12
- 1 Thessalonians 5:17-18

DAY 1

Spend Time with the Master
Identify a lust or desire over which you need God to help you win victory.

____

____

Live in the Word
Write the reference of your selected Scripture reading for today.

____

Write a thought from your Scripture reading to think about all day.

____

____

____

____

____

Pray in Faith
Obedience to God's Word is basic to your discipleship. Read the Bible passage again and write decisions you need to make to be obedient to the Word. Then pray about these decisions.

____

____

____

____

____

____

Fellowship with Believers

Choose an activity from the list on pages 165–68 to complete this week. Begin writing plans for completing it.

Witness to the World

Choose an activity from the list on pages 169–72 to complete this week. Begin writing plans for completing it.

Minister to Others

Choose an activity from the list on pages 173–76 to complete this week. Begin writing plans for completing it.

DAY 2

Spend Time with the Master
Write a quiet-time goal you are attempting to reach.

Live in the Word
Write the reference of your selected Scripture reading for today.

Complete the following sentence.

Living in the Word for me means—

Pray in Faith
Certain behavioral patterns develop when we continue certain sins. If you can see a pattern of sin in your life, you are probably in bondage to it. Describe this pattern of sin and ask God to release you from its bondage.

Fellowship with Believers

Record your progress in completing the activity you chose for this week.

Witness to the World

Record your progress in completing the activity you chose for this week.

Minister to Others

Record your progress in completing the activity you chose for this week.

DAY 3

Spend Time with the Master
Set a new goal for your quiet time.

Live in the Word
Write the reference of your selected Scripture reading for today.

Choose a doctrine taught in your Bible passage that you need to study further. Explain why you need to study it.

Pray in Faith
What percentage of your quiet time is used for prayer?

What percentage of your quiet time is used for reading the Bible?

Try to increase your emphasis on the area in which you are weaker.

Fellowship with Believers

Record your progress in completing the activity you chose for this week.

Witness to the World

Record your progress in completing the activity you chose for this week.

Minister to Others

Record your progress in completing the activity you chose for this week.

DAY 4

Spend Time with the Master

Identify a need in your family that only God can meet. Describe it below.

Live in the Word

Write the reference of your selected Scripture reading for today.

Recall a recent sermon that God has used to influence you. Describe how it has affected your life.

Pray in Faith

Recall things God has revealed to you that have saved you trouble or failure. You may have recorded these things in notes you kept on a sermon or in this journal. Review your notes for dates and warnings. Write these instances below.

Fellowship with Believers

Record your progress in completing the activity you chose for this week.

Witness to the World

Record your progress in completing the activity you chose for this week.

Minister to Others

Record your progress in completing the activity you chose for this week.

DAY 5

Spend Time with the Master
Complete one of the following sentences.

I will no longer ____

____

I need to be better at ____

____

I have come a long way in ____

____

I now have victory in ____

____

Live in the Word
Write the reference of your selected Scripture reading for today.

____

Distinguish between your living in the Word and the Word's living in you.

____

____

____

Pray in Faith
A regular prayer time emphasizes the increased value of listening to God. You may discover that listening to God is more valuable than talking to God. Which is more important for you today? Why?

____

____

Fellowship with Believers

Record your progress in completing the activity you chose for this week.

Witness to the World

Record your progress in completing the activity you chose for this week.

Minister to Others

Record your progress in completing the activity you chose for this week.

WEEK 4

Fellowship with Believers

J. DAVID CARTER

The Bible says: "You also, like living stones, are being built into a spiritual house to be a holy priesthood, offering spiritual sacrifices acceptable to God through Jesus Christ. You are a chosen people, a royal priesthood, a holy nation, a people belonging to God, that you may declare the praises of him who called you out of darkness into his wonderful light" (1 Pet. 2:5,9). Growing disciples need one another. Believers grow by being an active part of the body of Christ. Fellowship with other believers strengthens individual believers and the church to withstand Satan's attacks (see Matt. 16:18).

Fellowship with believers includes praise and thanksgiving to God (see 1 Pet. 2:9). Praise is adoring God for who He is. Thanksgiving is expressing gratitude to God for what He has done. Thanksgiving leads to praise. Growing disciples thank God in everything and continually praise Him. This is done individually and with other believers.

Christian fellowship involves gathering corporately for celebration, praise, encouragement, support, strength, and building relationships. Gathering places include homes, churches, businesses, large meeting halls, and conference/retreat centers. Believers gather as families, members of a congregation, participants in a focused activity, fellow workers, and members of a religious organization.

Fellowship with believers also provides a laboratory for Christian growth. Your personality might be tested, challenged, and strengthened by loving persons God gives you to love. To love others with the quality of love Christ taught requires change. We must discipline ourselves to forgive when we have been hurt, to seek reconciliation when we are not at fault, and to forgive and move on when the other person will not reconcile.

Fellowship with believers also carries a high degree of responsibility to one another and to God. Romans 15:1-5 says:

> We who are strong ought to bear with the failings of the weak and not to please ourselves. Each of us should please his neighbor for his good, to build him up. For even Christ did not please himself but, as it is written: "The insults of those who insult you have fallen on me." For everything that was written in the past was written to teach us, so that through endurance and the encouragement of the Scriptures we might have hope. May the God who

> gives endurance and encouragement give you a spirit of unity among yourselves as you follow Christ Jesus.

These instructions place a high degree of responsibility on each believer in the body of Christ. To live like this, we must be strong in our love for others and in our faith in God. We cannot live this way without maintaining a disciplined Christian life. If anything less than sacred or pure is in our lives, we are to confess it to God. We are to construct lives that reflect Jesus Christ.

Believers should not feel superior to one another. All have experienced the same kind of spiritual birth in Christ. Each one belongs to the household of faith because of his or her salvation by grace through faith. Each one grows in the faith by practicing the discipline of fellowshipping with other believers.

This Week's Suggested Scripture Readings

The following Scriptures support the discipline of fellowshipping with believers. Choose from these Scriptures to complete your "Live in the Word" assignment each day this week or substitute other Scriptures you have selected.

Day 1—Deuteronomy 12:24-27; John 11:5,35-36; 1 Thessalonians 5:12-15
Day 2—Psalm 84:4; John 15:12-17; 1 Timothy 5:17
Day 3—Micah 4:2; Acts 13:14-15; Hebrews 2:11; 1 Peter 2:9-10
Day 4—Mark 1:21; Romans 15:30; Hebrews 13:7; 1 John 1:3
Day 5—Luke 24:15,52-53; Galatians 4:4-7; 2 Corinthians 8:7; 1 Peter 4:8-9

This Week's Suggested Memory Verses

Memorize one of the following verses this week or another verse you have selected.

- John 15:12
- 1 Thessalonians 5:15
- John 15:16
- 1 Peter 2:9

DAY 1

Spend Time with the Master

Name someone to whom you could communicate the value of having a daily quiet time with God. Share your impressions with that person this week. Below write points you want to make.

____

____

____

Live in the Word

Write the reference of your selected Scripture reading for today.

____

"God speaks by the Holy Spirit through the Bible, prayer, circumstances, and the church to reveal Himself, His purposes, and His ways."[1] What did God say to you through the Bible today?

____

____

____

____

Pray in Faith

Ask God to show you an appropriate time and place to give a testimony of the value of using a journal. Write your prayer and answers to your prayer.

____

____

____

____

Fellowship with Believers

Choose an activity from the list on pages 165–68 to complete this week. Begin writing plans for completing it.

Witness to the World

Choose an activity from the list on pages 169–72 to complete this week. Begin writing plans for completing it.

Minister to Others

Choose an activity from the list on pages 173–76 to complete this week. Begin writing plans for completing it.

DAY 2

Spend Time with the Master

Compare the length of time you spend in your quiet time today with the time you normally spend. Write your opinion of what you discover.

Live in the Word

Write the reference of your selected Scripture reading for today.

As you read the Bible today, notice what is revealed about God's nature. Record your observations below.

Pray in Faith

You may notice that God uses several sources to tell you the same thing. When He does so, that message is important enough that He does not want you to miss it. Write a prayer that God will help you pay attention to what He is saying. Then pray your prayer to Him.

Fellowship with Believers

Record your progress in completing the activity you chose for this week.

Witness to the World

Record your progress in completing the activity you chose for this week.

Minister to Others

Record your progress in completing the activity you chose for this week.

DAY 3

Spend Time with the Master

Begin today's quiet time by praying, Lord, help me be sensitive to what You have been saying that I haven't heard.

Live in the Word

Write the reference of your selected Scripture reading for today.

____

Choose one verse to analyze today. Write each word separately. Beside each word write what it means to you. Ask God to help you see beyond the simple definitions of the words.

____

____

____

____

____

____

Pray in Faith

Use key words in the Bible passage you studied today to write a poemlike prayer.

____

____

____

____

____

____

Fellowship with Believers
Record your progress in completing the activity you chose for this week.

Witness to the World
Record your progress in completing the activity you chose for this week.

Minister to Others
Record your progress in completing the activity you chose for this week.

DAY 4

Spend Time with the Master

Look out a window long enough that you begin seeing things you normally do not see. Describe what you had to do to see these things. Compare that activity with what you must do to see spiritual realities or ministry needs that you do not readily see.

____

____

____

Live in the Word

Write the reference of your selected Scripture reading for today.

____

Look for a universal meaning or message in your Scripture passage. A universal meaning is one that applies at all times in all situations. For instance, the parable of the prodigal son teaches the value God places on wayward persons. Write the universal meaning you discover in today's passage.

____

____

____

Pray in Faith

Use your memory verse for this week as the basis for today's personal and intercessory prayers. Write notes below before praying.

____

____

____

____

Fellowship with Believers

Record your progress in completing the activity you chose for this week.

Witness to the World

Record your progress in completing the activity you chose for this week.

Minister to Others

Record your progress in completing the activity you chose for this week.

DAY 5

Spend Time with the Master

Other than a person, your health, or your job, what would be the most difficult things for you to lose? Beside each thing write the reason you listed it.

____

____

____

____

Live in the Word

Write the reference of your selected Scripture reading for today.

____

If you were teaching from today's passage, what would be the main idea to present?

____

____

____

____

Pray in Faith

We often have prayer requests that do not seem to be answered. Write the subject of one prayer you have prayed for a long time without an answer. Tell the Lord how you feel about this subject.

____

____

____

____

Fellowship with Believers

Record your progress in completing the activity you chose for this week.

Witness to the World

Record your progress in completing the activity you chose for this week.

Minister to Others

Record your progress in completing the activity you chose for this week.

---

[1]Henry T. Blackaby and Claude V. King, *Experiencing God: Knowing and Doing the Will of God* (Nashville: LifeWay Press, 1990), 20.

Witness to the World

J. DAVID CARTER

Witnessing is bearing spiritual fruit that identifies you as someone who walks with Jesus Christ. Witnessing is living a life that bears evidence of a strength that comes only from the Lord and draws others to Christ. Witnessing is also presenting the gospel of Jesus Christ. Following are some prerequisites for practicing the discipline of witnessing to the world.

Let Christ be Lord. The lordship of Christ is not a goal to reach; it is the position Christ holds in your life. This happens when you surrender the leadership of your life to Christ. Christ does not force you to turn over the control of your life to Him. The only way Christ can be Lord is by a voluntary act of your will.

The decision to make Christ Lord is also a decision no longer to do things your way. You want to know what Christ wants so that you can do things His way. This is why it is important to practice witnessing as a discipline. Witnessing is not automatic. Nothing in your nature would allow you to do that. A transformation has taken place. When Christ became Savior and Lord of your life, something happened in your spirit. A witness is one who gives testimony of what he or she has seen, heard, and knows. It is part of his or her life experiences. It is undeniable and certain. No one can talk you out of your testimony or take it from you. It is yours for eternity. God's Spirit works out this witness in us to give evidence that we are truly Christians: "The Spirit himself testifies with our spirit that we are God's children" (Rom. 8:16).

Develop Christlike character. "Do not conform any longer to the pattern of this world, but be transformed by the renewing of your mind. Then you will be able to test and approve what God's will is—his good, pleasing and perfect will" (Rom. 12:2). When a person accepts Christ as Savior and Lord, he or she will seek to replace un-Christlike character traits with Christlike character traits. Christ's characteristics can become part of a Christian's life when nurtured and encouraged. The person who wants to protect his rights will find that those rights are no longer important. Patience will replace frustration and struggle. Gentleness will replace selfishness and self-exaltation. Joy will replace the sadness of consistently having to fill life with activities to be happy. These changes are brought by Christ's transforming presence in our lives, not by our works.

When these virtues are present, a Christian will possess a strong and persuasive witness. Satan himself will back off if you exhibit God's authority and walk in the Spirit. You will experience victory because the Victor will fight the battles for you. You can go to Him in prayer and find strength beyond anything you can provide.

Have a change of will. As you walk with Christ, you will stop wanting what once drove you. Worldly desires will become empty. Because Christ is your Lord, you will find Him changing what you want. Things you thought essential will lose their appeal. You will recognize that your priorities are out of order, and you will seek God's help in reordering them. You will notice that the wrong priority has lost its attractiveness. Instead of buying something for yourself, you will experience the joy of giving.

God never forces His will on us, but He uses our experiences in life to cause us to be open to change. The experience may be one God initiated, or it may be a situation you got yourself into that He had to get you out of. Either way you decide: *Never again. I have learned my lesson. God, what would You have me do?*

As you gain confidence in the power of the Spirit of God living in you, you will find yourself talking about how your life has changed. This is a witness God will use to bring others to Him.

This Week's Suggested Scripture Readings

The following Scriptures support the discipline of witnessing to the world. Choose from these Scriptures to complete your "Live in the Word" assignment each day this week or substitute other Scriptures you have selected.

Day 1—Exodus 4:12; Matthew 9:37-38; Luke 21:14-15; John 20:21
Day 2—Psalm 22:27-28; Matthew 10:19; Acts 1:8; Ephesians 3:6
Day 3—Isaiah 9:2; Matthew 24:14; Acts 4:14; Ephesians 4:11
Day 4—Isaiah 45:22-25; Matthew 28:18-20; Acts 5:20-21; 2 Timothy 4:5
Day 5—Jeremiah 5:14; Mark 2:12; Acts 16:9-10; Philippians 2:10-11

This Week's Suggested Memory Verses

Memorize one of the following verses this week or another verse you have selected.

- Psalm 22:27-28
- Matthew 9:37-38
- Matthew 28:18-20
- Philippians 2:10-11

DAY 1

Spend Time with the Master

Keep a record of each time you turn to God for something today. Keep a record on a three-by-five-inch card and write the occasion, the time of day, and your immediate response. Plan to record this information in your journal tomorrow.

Live in the Word

Write the reference of your selected Scripture reading for today.

____

Write your memory verse for this week. Then underline each phrase or section of this verse as you meditate on it.

____

____

____

____

____

Pray in Faith

Express gratitude for the godly resources that have helped you through difficulty, trouble, and pain. Write your prayer here.

____

____

____

____

____

____

Fellowship with Believers

Choose an activity from the list on page 165–68 to complete this week. Begin writing plans for completing it.

Witness to the World

Choose an activity from the list on pages 169–72 to complete this week. Begin writing plans for completing it.

Minister to Others

Choose an activity from the list on pages 173–76 to complete this week. Begin writing plans for completing it.

DAY 2

Spend Time with the Master

Yesterday you were to keep a record of each time you turned to God for something. Below write the occasion, the time of day, and your immediate response each time you turned to God.

____

____

____

____

____

____

Live in the Word

Write the reference of your selected Scripture reading for today.

____

Record the passage on a piece of paper or on a card to refer to throughout the day.

Pray in Faith

Choose a family member or a friend and think of that person's activities and circumstances. Ask God how you can be a prayer warrior for this person. Write your impressions below. Use part of your prayer time today interceding in prayer for that person.

____

____

____

____

____

Fellowship with Believers

Record your progress in completing the activity you chose for this week.

Witness to the World

Record your progress in completing the activity you chose for this week.

Minister to Others

Record your progress in completing the activity you chose for this week.

DAY 3

Spend Time with the Master
Write the reference of your selected Scripture reading for today.

____

Read your Scripture for today, choose two or three key words, and write them below. Beside each word describe in one sentence why you consider the word significant.

____

____

____

____

Live in the Word
Write a summary of what God said to you today through the Scripture you read.

____

____

____

____

____

Pray in Faith
Update and maintain your prayer lists for daily, weekly, and monthly concerns (pp. 178–79). Choose one prayer need from your monthly list and include it in today's prayer time. Write notes about it below.

____

____

Fellowship with Believers

Record your progress in completing the activity you chose for this week.

Witness to the World

Record your progress in completing the activity you chose for this week.

Minister to Others

Record your progress in completing the activity you chose for this week.

DAY 4

Spend Time with the Master

Recall a key memorized Scripture and write it below. As you write it, recall the occasion that caused you to memorize it. Express gratitude to God for the message of this verse.

____

____

____

____

Live in the Word

Write the reference of your selected Scripture reading for today.

____

List two or three ways you can apply today's Scripture passage to your life.

____

____

____

____

Pray in Faith

Choose several prayer needs from your weekly prayer list (p. 179) and include them in today's prayer time. Describe them below.

____

____

____

____

Fellowship with Believers

Record your progress in completing the activity you chose for this week.

Witness to the World

Record your progress in completing the activity you chose for this week.

Minister to Others

Record your progress in completing the activity you chose for this week.

DAY 5

Spend Time with the Master

Often, God does not work on our schedule. Describe an occasion when you were glad He worked on His schedule, not yours.

Have you kept records of spiritual markers—special times in your life when God taught you more about Himself in order to increase your faith? Consider recording spiritual markers on page 180 of this journal.

Live in the Word

Write the reference of your selected Scripture reading for today.

Read today's passage at least five times. After reading it, meditate on what God is saying to you. Write a summary of what God says.

Pray in Faith

Kneel and pray with your head raised and your hands open, palms up, to talk and listen to God. Write the way this attitude affected your prayers.

Fellowship with Believers

Record your progress in completing the activity you chose for this week.

Witness to the World

Record your progress in completing the activity you chose for this week.

Minister to Others

Record your progress in completing the activity you chose for this week.

Minister to Others

AVERY T. WILLIS, JR.

Every disciple is to minister to others in Jesus' name. To fail to minister is to thwart God's purpose for you. Jesus made it plain: " 'Whoever serves me must follow me; and where I am, my servant also will be. My Father will honor the one who serves me' " (John 12:26). He also taught, " 'A student is not above his teacher, but everyone who is fully trained will be like his teacher' " (Luke 6:40). If we follow Jesus, we will minister.

The example of the early church gives us an outline of serving others through various ministries. Scripture describes those ministries like this:

> They devoted themselves to the apostles' teaching and to the fellowship, to the breaking of bread and to prayer. Everyone was filled with awe, and many wonders and miraculous signs were done by the apostles. All the believers were together and had everything in common. Selling their possessions and goods, they gave to anyone as he had need. Every day they continued to meet together in the temple courts. They broke bread in their homes and ate together with glad and sincere hearts, praising God and enjoying the favor of all the people. And the Lord added to their number daily those who were being saved (Acts 2:42-47).

First, the early believers ministered through preaching and teaching. Peter preached at Pentecost, and all of the disciples taught. The ones they trained, such as Philip and Stephen, also taught. The ministry of teaching and preaching is the skeleton of the body of Christ that gives it shape and strength.

Second, they ministered in worship and intercession. Every day they worshiped in the temple and in homes, praising God with glad and sincere hearts. This pattern continued when they were threatened with prison and persecution: "Peter was kept in prison, but the church was earnestly praying to God for him" (Acts 12:5). God heard their intercession and delivered Peter from prison. The ministry of worship and intercession gives the body of Christ fresh life.

Third, they ministered by nurturing new believers. The disciples discipled those who had repented and believed in Jesus as Savior and Lord. They fellowshipped with them and helped them grow as Christians. They solved their disputes. They taught them how to worship. They showed them how to share their possessions with fellow Christians. The ministry of nurture provides an environment for the body of Christ to grow.

Fourth, they ministered in evangelism. God added to the church daily those who were being saved by their witness. The ministry of evangelism causes the body of Christ to multiply as God blesses through the ministry of witness.

Fifth, they ministered to the needy by selling their possessions and sharing equally with all of the believers. Everyone had what he or she needed. The ministry of service gives the body of Christ away to those in need.

You are a minister. First Peter 2:9 says, "You are a chosen people, a royal priesthood, a holy nation, a people belonging to God, that you may declare the praises of him who called you out of darkness into his wonderful light." God never intended for us to be a reservoir of His blessings but a channel for them to flow to others. He gave whatever He has given you so that you can share it with others. As He blesses others through you, you experience the delight of doing the Father's will. Use whatever God has given you to minister to others.

This Week's Suggested Scripture Readings

The following Scriptures support the discipline of ministering to others. Choose from these Scriptures to complete your "Live in the Word" assignment each day this week or substitute other Scriptures you have selected.

Day 1—Judges 5:2; Matthew 5:13-16; 1 Corinthians 3:9; 2 Timothy 4:2

Day 2—Deuteronomy 10:12; Matthew 25:22-23; 1 Corinthians 15:58; Titus 2:7

Day 3—Psalm 40:8; Mark 10:43-45; 2 Corinthians 6:1; Hebrews 10:24

Day 4—Luke 10:25-37; John 13:14-16; Galatians 6:10; James 4:17

Day 5—Luke 12:48; John 21:15-17; Ephesians 4:11-12; 1 Peter 4:10-11

This Week's Suggested Memory Verses

Memorize one of the following verses this week or another verse you have selected.

- Deuteronomy 10:12
- Matthew 5:16
- 1 Corinthians 15:58
- Hebrews 10:24

DAY 1

Spend Time with the Master

Write the present time of day: ______________________________

What plans do you have 12 hours from now? If you face something unexpected and painful, what resource do you plan to turn to for help?

____

____

Live in the Word

Write the reference of your selected Scripture reading for today.

____

"God is always at work around you."[1] What is God saying through today's Scripture to invite you to join Him in that work?

____

____

____

____

Pray in Faith

Ask God to heal you of any hindrance that prevents you from being totally obedient. Write your prayer here.

____

____

____

____

____

Fellowship with Believers

Choose an activity from the list on pages 165–68 to complete this week. Begin writing plans for completing it.

Witness to the World

Choose an activity from the list on pages 169–72 to complete this week. Begin writing plans for completing it.

Minister to Others

Choose an activity from the list on pages 173–76 to complete this week. Begin writing plans for completing it.

DAY 2

Spend Time with the Master

Choose a family member or a friend and think of that person's activities and circumstances. Ask God how you can be a prayer warrior for this person. Write your impressions below.

____

____

____

____

Live in the Word

Write the reference of your selected Scripture reading for today.

____

Regular Bible reading identifies areas of our lives in which we must make adjustments to join God in His work. Name one area of your life in which you recognize a need for adjustment.

____

____

Pray in Faith

Ask God for the strength to make the necessary adjustments to join Him in His work. Write your prayer below.

____

____

____

____

____

Fellowship with Believers

Record your progress in completing the activity you chose for this week.

Witness to the World

Record your progress in completing the activity you chose for this week.

Minister to Others

Record your progress in completing the activity you chose for this week.

DAY 3

Spend Time with the Master
Review your plans for an extended time with God during or after week 13 (see pp. 153–54). Write the date, time, and place you have planned.

Live in the Word
Write the reference of your selected Scripture reading for today.

The Bible instructs us to live a disciplined Christian life. Write one discipline you need to be stronger in your faith. Explain why you named that discipline.

Pray in Faith
Ask God to show you why it is difficult for you to establish the discipline mentioned in "Live in the Word." Write your prayer below. Continue including this need in your prayers until you discover the answer. You may want to add this to your daily, weekly, or monthly prayer list (pp. 178–79).

Fellowship with Believers
Record your progress in completing the activity you chose for this week.

Witness to the World
Record your progress in completing the activity you chose for this week.

Minister to Others
Record your progress in completing the activity you chose for this week.

DAY 4

SPEND TIME WITH THE MASTER

Review your journal notes for week 2. Identify a prayer need in that week and write a progress statement below.

____

____

____

LIVE IN THE WORD

Write the reference of your selected Scripture reading for today.

____

God's Word provides help for maintaining self-control. Recall a Scripture you have memorized that has helped you maintain self-control. Write that Scripture below.

____

____

____

____

PRAY IN FAITH

Praying without ceasing will help you maintain self-control because it brings Spirit control. Name an area of your life needing greater Spirit control. Write a prayer in which you yield to the Spirit's control. Then pray.

____

____

____

____

Fellowship with Believers

Record your progress in completing the activity you chose for this week.

Witness to the World

Record your progress in completing the activity you chose for this week.

Minister to Others

Record your progress in completing the activity you chose for this week.

DAY 5

Spend Time with the Master
Write the name of a person who means a great deal to you. List from three to five characteristics of that person you most admire. During the next week write this person a note expressing the value of your relationship.

Live in the Word
Write the reference of your selected Scripture reading for today.

On day 1 of week 2 you began being alert to a life verse God might reveal to you. Write the reference below and record a way that verse has contributed to your life.

Pray in Faith
Rewrite your life verse in the form of a prayer. Then pray it to God.

Fellowship with Believers

Record your progress in completing the activity you chose for this week.

____

____

____

____

Witness to the World

Record your progress in completing the activity you chose for this week.

____

____

____

____

Minister to Others

Record your progress in completing the activity you chose for this week.

____

____

____

____

You are almost halfway through *Day by Day in God's Kingdom.* Order another copy now so that you will be ready to begin using it after you complete this journal. Order item 0-7673-2577-X from the Customer Service Center; 127 Ninth Avenue, North; Nashville, TN 37234; 1-800-458-2772; or visit a Baptist Book Store or a Lifeway Christian Store.

WEEK 7

SPEND TIME WITH THE MASTER

†

AVERY T. WILLIS, JR.

Jesus called His disciples to " 'come, follow me' " (Matt. 4:19). More than anything else, Jesus wanted to spend time with His disciples. He knew that being with Him in all kinds of situations would equip the disciples to do that for which He had chosen them. They soon learned the truth of John 15:5: " 'I am the vine; you are the branches. If a man remains in me and I in him, he will bear much fruit; apart from me you can do nothing.' "

A disciple is one who follows Jesus, learns from Him, and obeys Him as Lord. Jesus wants to spend time with you. Only by staying in contact with Him can you do that for which He has chosen you. The single most important way to spend time with the Master and learn to follow Him is to have a quiet time every day, in which you meet Him through Bible reading and prayer. A quiet time is not just a habit or just a few quick minutes spent in prayer and the Word. A quiet time is a time when you are still and know that He is God. It is a time when you listen to God. God's Word is the primary way God speaks to you.

You need to hear all of God's counsel. Here are a few suggestions for hearing all God is saying to you in your quiet time.

1. *Allow enough time to read His Word reflectively.* God told Joshua: " 'Meditate on it day and night, so that you may be careful to do everything written in it. Then you will be prosperous and successful' " (Josh. 1:8). Do not try to read so much Scripture at one time that you cannot meditate on its meaning and let God speak directly to you and your situation. To spend time with the Master, continue to meditate on the Word at all times. The psalmist said:

   > His delight is in the law of the Lord,
   >   and on his law he meditates day and night.
   > He is like a tree planted by streams of water,
   >   which yields its fruit in season and whose leaf
   >   does not wither (Ps. 1:2-3).

2. *Balance your reading of the Word.* Jesus said, " 'Everything must be fulfilled that is written about me in the Law of Moses, the Prophets and the Psalms.' Then he opened their minds so they could understand the Scriptures" (Luke 24:44-45). These three designations of Scripture cover all of the Old Testament, which was the Bible Jesus used. Be sure to vary your

reading so that all of God's counsel is available to you. You may read the Bible from Genesis to Revelation over a year's time or each day read part of the Old Testament and part of the New Testament. You may prefer to read a book of the Bible at a time and then go to another book of a different type.

3. *Apply the Word to your life each day.* Revelation 1:3 says, "Blessed is the one who reads the words of this prophecy, and blessed are those who hear it and take to heart what is written in it, because the time is near." When you take it to heart, you ask God to show you what it means to you and your life. Jesus promised that " 'if you obey my commands, you will remain in my love, just as I have obeyed my Father's commands and remain in his love' " (John 15:10). Every time you apply God's Word to your life, you grow closer to Him.

After you have heard His Word, you are prepared to respond to it in prayer and obedience. Jesus said: " 'If anyone loves me, he will obey my teaching. My Father will love him, and we will come to him and make our home with him' " (John 14:23). Time spent with God is the most delightful time of the day.

This Week's Suggested Scripture Readings

The following Scriptures support the discipline of spending time with the Master. Choose from these Scriptures to complete your "Live in the Word" assignment each day this week or substitute other Scriptures you have selected.

Day 1—Psalm 55:17; 1 Timothy 5:5
Day 2—Psalm 119:147; 1 John 1:3
Day 3—Daniel 6:10; Revelation 3:20
Day 4—Matthew 18:20; Psalm 77:1-2
Day 5—Mark 1:35; Luke 2:37

This Week's Suggested Memory Verses

Memorize one of the following verses this week or another verse you have selected.

- Psalm 55:17
- Matthew 18:20

DAY 1

SPEND TIME WITH THE MASTER

As you spend time with the Master, try kneeling. Do this during your quiet time each day this week. If physical limitations prevent this, imagine that you are on your knees during your quiet time. Write the way this attitude affects your quiet time today.

____

____

____

LIVE IN THE WORD

Write your selected Scripture reading for today. Underline or highlight the key words in the passage. Choose three or more of these words and beside each write a statement describing how it applies to your life.

____

____

____

____

____

____

____

____

____

____

PRAY IN FAITH

Use the key words identified in "Live in the Word" in sentence prayers.

Fellowship with Believers

Choose an activity from the list on pages 165–68 to complete this week. Begin writing plans for completing it.

Witness to the World

Choose an activity from the list on pages 169–72 to complete this week. Begin writing plans for completing it.

Minister to Others

Choose an activity from the list on pages 173–76 to complete this week. Begin writing plans for completing it.

DAY 2

Spend Time with the Master

Ask yourself, *Am I abiding in Christ?* Read John 15:10 and write what is required to abide in Christ.

____

____

____

Live in the Word

Write the reference of your selected Scripture reading for today.

____

Outline the passage's main ideas.

____

____

____

____

____

Pray in Faith

Referring to "Spend Time with the Master" in week 1, day 1, read your description of what your quiet time means to you. List and express your feelings of gratitude for the benefits you have received from having a quiet time.

____

____

____

____

Fellowship with Believers

Record your progress in completing the activity you chose for this week.

Witness to the World

Record your progress in completing the activity you chose for this week.

Minister to Others

Record your progress in completing the activity you chose for this week.

DAY 3

Spend Time with the Master

Select one of God's commandments you have difficulty practicing. Write it below. Be attentive throughout the day to a word from God about the reason you may have trouble obeying His command.

____

____

____

Live in the Word

Write the reference of your selected Scripture reading for today.

____

Use the cross-references or footnotes in your Bible to locate a related passage. Write a statement that describes the similarity between the two passages.

____

____

____

____

Pray in Faith

Pray for all of the unsaved persons your life will potentially touch today. Ask God to help you be and say what will exalt Him and that He will help you present the gospel to them. First write your thoughts here.

____

____

____

____

Fellowship with Believers

Record your progress in completing the activity you chose for this week.

Witness to the World

Record your progress in completing the activity you chose for this week.

Minister to Others

Record your progress in completing the activity you chose for this week.

DAY 4

Spend Time with the Master

Spending time with the Master is a 24-hour-a-day process. Ask yourself: *Am I aware of God's presence throughout the day? How?* Answer below.

____

____

____

Live in the Word

Write the reference of your selected Scripture reading for today.

____

Describe what it means to you to read God's Word daily.

____

____

____

____

Write a note to your pastor and tell him what you wrote. Also express your gratitude for the sermons he prepares.

Pray in Faith

Recall all of the pastors and staff members who have ministered to you and have influenced your life. List their names below. Pray for them and their families. Some may already be in heaven. Thank God for using them in your life.

____

____

____

____

Fellowship with Believers

Record your progress in completing the activity you chose for this week.

Witness to the World

Record your progress in completing the activity you chose for this week.

Minister to Others

Record your progress in completing the activity you chose for this week.

DAY 5

Spend Time with the Master

Sit with your hands palms up for a while to illustrate your openness to receive from God. Afterward, write a sentence that describes your attitude.

Live in the Word

Write the reference of your selected Scripture reading for today.

God has a way of calling our attention to a special passage of Scripture. Review your notes for the past two or three weeks and recall when God seemed to shine a light on a particular passage. What was that passage? What does that passage say to you today?

Pray in Faith

Ask God to remind you of one or more persons with whom you need reconciliation. List their names below. Jesus washed others' feet and allowed His feet to be washed. Imagine that you are washing the feet of one of the persons you identified and are allowing yours to be washed. Ask God to cleanse your heart and to help you take action to reconcile your relationships.

Fellowship with Believers

Record your progress in completing the activity you chose for this week.

Witness to the World

Record your progress in completing the activity you chose for this week.

Minister to Others

Record your progress in completing the activity you chose for this week.

Live in the Word

AVERY T. WILLIS, JR.

God wants you to be like Him and to join Him in His work. The Holy Spirit is at work building your character in the likeness of Christ. His primary tool is God's Word: "All Scripture is God-breathed and is useful for teaching, rebuking, correcting and training in righteousness, so that the man of God may be thoroughly equipped for every good work" (2 Tim. 3:16-17). Here are four ways God uses the Word to shape you into His image.

1. *God uses the Word to teach you.* He wants you to know truth. Jesus prayed to the Father, " 'Your word is truth' " (John 17:17). As you study about God and His acts, the Holy Spirit creates a desire in you to be like the Father and the Son. As you study doctrine, you learn the foundations of the faith. As you live in the Word, you learn the results of right and wrong actions. God also teaches you about Himself. The psalmist said:

   Teach me, O Lord, to follow your decrees;
   then I will keep them to the end.
   Give me understanding, and I will keep your law
   and obey it with all my heart (Ps. 119:33-34).

2. *God uses the Word to rebuke you when you depart from His teaching.* He knows all you do and think and why you think it. God warns us; if we do not respond to His voice, He must rebuke us with His acts. The psalmist said,

   I know, O Lord, that your laws are righteous,
   and in faithfulness you have afflicted me (Ps. 119:75).

   God's Word will return you to God:

   Before I was afflicted I went astray,
   but now I obey your word (Ps. 119:67).

3. *God uses the Word to correct you when you stray from His teaching.* Correcting is not the same as rebuking. A rebuke comes when you have gone the wrong way. Correction comes when you have strayed from the path. The psalmist expressed it:

> I have strayed like a lost sheep.
> Seek your servant,
> for I have not forgotten your commands (Ps. 119:176).

When you begin to veer from the path, He gently nudges you back on the right road. Do as the psalmist did:

> I have considered my ways
> and have turned my steps to your statutes.
> I will hasten and not delay
> to obey your commands (Ps. 119:59-60).

4. *God uses the Word to instruct you in righteousness even before you go astray.*

> Your word is a lamp to my feet
> and a light for my path (Ps. 119:105).

Pray with the psalmist:

> Direct me in the path of your commands,
> for there I find delight.
> Turn my heart toward your statutes
> and not toward selfish gain.
> Turn my eyes away from worthless things;
> preserve my life according to your word (Ps. 119:35-37).

This Week's Suggested Scripture Readings

The following Scriptures support the discipline of living in the Word. Choose from these Scriptures to complete your "Live in the Word" assignment each day this week or substitute other Scriptures you have selected.

Day 1—Deuteronomy 6:6-9; Proverbs 29:18; Luke 21:33
Day 2—Joshua 23:6; Psalm 119:130; Isaiah 40:8; John 8:31
Day 3—Psalm 37:31; Psalm 119:140-148; Jeremiah 31:33; Romans 15:4
Day 4—Psalm 40:8; Matthew 4:4; Hebrews 4:12
Day 5—Psalm 119:7-9,11,89,97; 1 John 5:13; Revelation 1:3

This Week's Suggested Memory Verses

Memorize one of the following verses this week or another verse you have selected.

- Psalm 40:8
- Psalm 119:11
- Luke 21:33
- Hebrews 4:12

DAY 1

Spend Time with the Master
Write any hindrances to being totally obedient. Ask God to remove them.

Live in the Word
Write the reference of your selected Scripture reading for today.

What was the most meaningful verse you read today? Write it below.

Pray in Faith
Pray for the immediate members of your family. List their names below as you pray for them. All of your family members' names should be on your daily, weekly, or monthly prayer list (pp. 178–79). If you have not added them, do so now.

Fellowship with Believers

Choose an activity from the list on pages 165–68 to complete this week. Begin writing plans for completing it.

Witness to the World

Choose an activity from the list on pages 169–72 to complete this week. Begin writing plans for completing it.

Minister to Others

Choose an activity from the list on pages 173–76 to complete this week. Begin writing plans for completing it.

DAY 2

Spend Time with the Master

Name a family member or a friend for whom you are praying and in whose life you feel changes are not happening fast enough. Explain this situation below. Ask God to show you what He is doing in this person's life.

____

____

____

Live in the Word

Write the reference of your selected Scripture reading for today.

____

What is God asking you to do as you read your Scripture?

____

____

____

____

Pray in Faith

Prayer is not just a religious activity; it is conversation with Almighty God. Begin your prayer time today by addressing Him as Almighty God. Complete this sentence:

Almighty God, I—

____

____

____

____

Fellowship with Believers

Record your progress in completing the activity you chose for this week.

Witness to the World

Record your progress in completing the activity you chose for this week.

Minister to Others

Record your progress in completing the activity you chose for this week.

DAY 3

Spend Time with the Master
Remember vows you made to God during a difficult time. If you need to renew a vow, do it now. Write your prayer below.

____

____

____

Live in the Word
Write the reference of your selected Scripture reading for today.

____

God gives Scripture for teaching. What did you learn today in your Scripture reading?

____

____

____

____

____

Pray in Faith
One type of prayer is praise. While thanksgiving primarily calls attention to God's activity, praise primarily calls attention to God's nature. References to praise in the Bible often mention God's names. A good prayer activity is to recall the things God does for you. Then pray to Him, using a name that relates to one of His actions.

Many names for Jesus are used in the Bible. Today recall one of these names and pray based on what it represents to you.

Example: Jesus said, " 'I have called you friends' " (John 15:15). My Friend, I am glad I can count on You during this lonely time.

Fellowship with Believers

Record your progress in completing the activity you chose for this week.

Witness to the World

Record your progress in completing the activity you chose for this week.

Minister to Others

Record your progress in completing the activity you chose for this week.

DAY 4

Spend Time with the Master

Identify any unacceptable pattern in your life. Identify the opposite of that pattern. Describe what you need to do to change the unacceptable pattern.

Live in the Word

Write the reference of your selected Scripture reading for today.

God gives Scripture for instruction. What instructions did you receive today?

Pray in Faith

When God gives instructions, He wants us to acknowledge them with an obedient response. Write and pray a prayer in which you submit to His instructions.

Fellowship with Believers

Record your progress in completing the activity you chose for this week.

Witness to the World

Record your progress in completing the activity you chose for this week.

Minister to Others

Record your progress in completing the activity you chose for this week.

DAY 5

Spend Time with the Master

Be attentive to at least two persons in whom you see spiritual needs. Write the names and the spiritual needs below. Then add the persons' names to your weekly and monthly prayer lists (p. 179).

____

____

____

____

Live in the Word

Write the reference of your selected Scripture reading for today.

____

God gives Scripture for correction. What corrections do you need to make in your life?

____

____

____

Pray in Faith

God provides directions for us through the Bible. Prayer is our response to the directions He gives us. Write a prayer expressing your desire to follow His directions.

____

____

____

____

Fellowship with Believers

Record your progress in completing the activity you chose for this week.

Witness to the World

Record your progress in completing the activity you chose for this week.

Minister to Others

Record your progress in completing the activity you chose for this week.

WEEK 9

Pray in Faith

J. DAVID CARTER

"Faith is the substance of things hoped for, the evidence of things not seen" (Heb. 11:1, KJV). This often-quoted verse suggests that if you have faith, you have the substance and the evidence to prove it. Just because you can't see something doesn't mean it is not there. Faith is believing God enough to count on what He says. If God says He will do something, you can count on it: " 'Whatever you ask for in prayer, believe that you have received it, and it will be yours' " (Mark 11:24). As you walk in fellowship with the Lord Jesus, you will discover that He is always looking out for you. In fact, Christ knows what is best for you.

In order to desire the kinds of things Jesus wants us to have, we have to work through and remove a lot of distractions, fears, sins, and other obstacles. When these things are out of the way, we can clearly hear what Jesus is saying to us. The desires of our hearts will change. We discover that Jesus has always wanted us to have the best, but we were deceived to believe that all of the great things in life were somewhere else. As we remove these distractions, Jesus replaces them with an abundant life. We may not possess all of the material things in this world or achieve worldly success, but because of our faith relationship with Christ, those things don't matter.

Jesus said, " 'If ye abide in me, and my words abide in you, ye shall ask what ye will, and it shall be done unto you' " (John 15:7, KJV). This is one of the most open promises in the Bible. Jesus gives two qualifications: "if you abide in Me" and "if My words abide in you." Together the two define our relationship with Jesus. The position of abiding is one in which faithfulness replaces distrust, love replaces selfishness, peace replaces entertainment, patience replaces frustration, and joy replaces sadness. This abiding relationship is based on our obedience to God's will.

The person who prays in faith has decided that it is better to do it God's way. Many times we may not understand God's way, and sometimes God doesn't even tell us why. Even so, it is by asking why that we draw closer to God. Once we begin seeing God as One who is interested in the welfare of our lives and souls, we will no longer see Him as a heavenly banker to whom we can make requests to meet our desires. What God wants to give us cannot be bought with cash or put on a credit card. What God wants for us has been eternally paid for by Jesus.

The best way to strengthen our faith is to strengthen our relationship with God. We do this by being in the Word in such a way that our prayers of faith express what we know to be God's will. The Bible tells us that our faith doesn't have to be any larger than a grain of mustard seed (see Matt. 17:20). Faith is believing God and taking Him at His word. Praying in faith is communicating with the only One who loves us enough to die for us. That should be enough to deepen and sustain our faith.

This Week's Suggested Scripture Readings

The following Scriptures support the discipline of praying in faith. Choose from these Scriptures to complete your "Live in the Word" assignment each day this week or substitute other Scriptures you have selected.

Day 1—Psalm 88:1-2; Matthew 7:7-8; Philippians 4:6
Day 2—Psalm 9:1-2; Matthew 21:21-22; James 5:13-16
Day 3—Psalm 37:5-6; Matthew 7:9-11; Romans 8:26-27
Day 4—Psalm 103; Luke 18:1-8
Day 5—Job 19:25; Proverbs 3:5-6; Ephesians 6:18

This Week's Suggested Memory Verses

Memorize one of the following verses this week or another verse you have selected.

- Proverbs 3:5-6
- Matthew 7:7-8
- Philippians 4:6
- James 5:16

DAY 1

Spend Time with the Master
Your quiet time is an appointment with God. Describe the value your quiet time holds for you.

Live in the Word
Write the reference of your selected Scripture reading for today.

God gives Scripture for reproof. Reproof is strong correction when you depart from God's teaching. Does any activity in your life require reproof? ❑ Yes ❑ No If so, why do you hold to it?

Pray in Faith
God increases His discipline until He gets our attention. Ask God to show you areas of your life needing correction before He must use reproof. Record what He shows you.

Fellowship with Believers

Choose an activity from the list on pages 165–68 to complete this week. Begin writing plans for completing it.

Witness to the World

Choose an activity from the list on pages 169–72 to complete this week. Begin writing plans for completing it.

Minister to Others

Choose an activity from the list on pages 173–76 to complete this week. Begin writing plans for completing it.

DAY 2

Spend Time with the Master
As you consider God's activity in your life for the past few weeks, can you see a pattern developing? ❑ Yes ❑ No Describe that pattern. If you have difficulty identifying a pattern, ask God to help you see it.

____

____

Live in the Word
Write the reference of your selected Scripture reading for today.

____

Hiding God's Word in our hearts prevents us from sinning. What sins have you avoided because God's Word is in your heart?

____

Pray in Faith
Recall several Bible verses you have memorized. Write them as prayers asking God to renew and heal your spirit as you quote them.

____

____

____

____

____

____

____

____

____

Fellowship with Believers

Record your progress in completing the activity you chose for this week.

Witness to the World

Record your progress in completing the activity you chose for this week.

Minister to Others

Record your progress in completing the activity you chose for this week.

DAY 3

Spend Time with the Master

During your quiet time add a new emphasis to your prayer time. Write something you will include in your prayer time that you have not previously mentioned—either a new subject or a different type of prayer, such as confession, thanksgiving, or praise.

____

____

Live in the Word

Write the reference of your selected Scripture reading for today.

____

The Word gives light to our path. Where is God's Word shining in your life to direct you on the right path?

____

____

____

____

____

Pray in Faith

Write the areas of your life in which major as well as minor decisions must be made. Ask God to give you the light of His wisdom to know what to do and the best time to do it.

____

____

____

____

Fellowship with Believers
Record your progress in completing the activity you chose for this week.

Witness to the World
Record your progress in completing the activity you chose for this week.

Minister to Others
Record your progress in completing the activity you chose for this week.

DAY 4

SPEND TIME WITH THE MASTER

During your quiet time today ask God to show you work He is trying to do in which you have not joined Him. Write the excuses you have used, if any.

LIVE IN THE WORD

Write the reference of your selected Scripture reading for today.

Without the Holy Spirit to teach us, we cannot receive a spiritual meaning from Scripture. Ask the Holy Spirit to help you understand the spiritual meaning of your passage today. Write it here.

PRAY IN FAITH

Ask God to open your understanding to a deeper level of insight to receive what God has for you. Write your prayer.

Fellowship with Believers

Record your progress in completing the activity you chose for this week.

Witness to the World

Record your progress in completing the activity you chose for this week.

Minister to Others

Record your progress in completing the activity you chose for this week.

DAY 5

Spend Time with the Master

Review the excuses you wrote yesterday. List actions you need to take to stop making excuses and join God's work.

Live in the Word

Write the reference of your selected Scripture reading for today.

Summarize what God says to you through your Scripture passage.

Pray in Faith

Today use your prayer time to listen. Read the notes you made for the past nine days and review what God said. Identify something you should believe, do, learn more about, or share with others.

Fellowship with Believers
Record your progress in completing the activity you chose for this week.

Witness to the World
Record your progress in completing the activity you chose for this week.

Minister to Others
Record your progress in completing the activity you chose for this week.

WEEK 10

Fellowship with Believers

J. DAVID CARTER

Christians make a covenant with God. When you make an agreement with God, it is eternal. This relationship with the Lord brings us together as a covenant community of fellow Christians—a church. Our relationships with Christians extend beyond the doors of our own church building to those in other churches. A network of support exists among all believers in Christ.

The discipline of fellowshipping with believers builds strong relationships. Believers share victories and struggles. They depend on, support, and encourage one another. They cry when others cry and laugh when others laugh.

Our fellowship is one of love. We relate to other believers because we love God and one another. Genuine Christian fellowship includes a commitment to love those who share faith in Jesus Christ. Jesus said: " 'A new command I give you: Love one another. As I have loved you, so you must love one another. By this all men will know that you are my disciples' " (John 13:34-35). Jesus wants believers to experience the quality of love for one another that we have with Him. Christ loved all kinds of persons with all kinds of needs. We are to do the same.

Why is fellowshipping with believers a discipline? Because it costs us to love others. Love is not given without self-denial. Loving others costs time, disappointment, disillusionment, risk, trust, and more. In our relationship with Christ we receive the spiritual strength to continue loving when we don't feel like loving. Jesus' command in John 13:34-35 is not optional. We are to do it whether or not our hearts are in it. We are to follow this command in obedience. But Jesus wants us to go farther. We are to get our hearts into it: " 'You must love one another.' "

Our relationship with Christ enables us to love to the point of bearing one another's burden and carrying one another's load. Fellowship provides support, leadership, accountability, strength, encouragement, and direction for a unified mission. Some people go to church for what they can get out of it. Their faithfulness and loyalty are in direct proportion to the way their needs are met. The discipline of fellowshipping with believers shifts their focus from their needs to the needs of others. They are encouraged to move from only using the spiritual gifts of others to letting God use their gifts in ministry to others. When this happens, they become ministers, fulfilling God's redemptive work in the world.

A nurturing, caring church attracts persons looking for Christlike love. Unbelievers and persons in crisis are drawn to a church whose members express loving support and ministry. Fellowship among believers is to be steadfast in teaching God's truths and in sharing with one another (see Acts 2:42,44-45). It is not unusual to find that generosity characterizes a church in which the discipline of fellowshipping with believers is given high priority. Acts 2:46 tells us that the early believers regularly met together corporately and in homes. This was their lifestyle. The result was a singleness of heart, expressed in their growing fellowship with God and other believers. May you find the same in your fellowship with other believers.

This Week's Suggested Scripture Readings

The following Scriptures support the discipline of fellowshipping with believers. Choose from these Scriptures to complete your "Live in the Word" assignment each day this week or substitute other Scriptures you have selected.

Day 1—Deuteronomy 14:2; Acts 2:42-47; 1 Corinthians 10:16-17
Day 2—Psalm 119:63; Romans 1:12; Hebrews 10:25; 1 Peter 2:17
Day 3—Malachi 3:16; 1 Corinthians 16:15-18; Ephesians 2:19-22; 1 John 1:6-7
Day 4—Psalm 122:1; Luke 4:16; Romans 15:5-6; Ephesians 4:2-3
Day 5—John 1:12; Philippians 1:3-6; Philippians 2:1-4

This Week's Suggested Memory Verses

Memorize one of the following verses this week or another verse you have selected.

- Psalm 122:1
- Hebrews 10:25
- Philippians 2:3
- 1 John 1:7

DAY 1

Spend Time with the Master

It is usually easier to keep a record of what we are doing for God than of what God is doing for us. Name at least five things God is doing for you.

Live in the Word

Write the reference of your selected Scripture reading for today.

When you read the Bible, you are listening to God. What is God's Word saying to you today?

Pray in Faith

Write and express your gratitude to God for the Bible. Think of specific reasons you are thankful, such as: I thank You, God, for the time You gave me a promise verse.

Fellowship with Believers

Choose an activity from the list on pages 165–68 to complete this week. Begin writing plans for completing it.

Witness to the World

Choose an activity from the list on pages 169–72 to complete this week. Begin writing plans for completing it.

Minister to Others

Choose an activity from the list on pages 173–76 to complete this week. Begin writing plans for completing it.

DAY 2

Spend Time with the Master

Refer to your journal notes from yesterday, when you named five things God is doing for you. Allow God to show you why He is doing those things. Write at least one reason below.

____

____

____

Live in the Word

Write the reference of your selected Scripture reading for today.

____

As you read your Bible today, imagine that the Lord is seated across from you speaking the things you are reading. Listen to Him as you read. Record what He says to you.

____

____

____

Pray in Faith

Continue considering that the Lord is seated across from you. Write a prayer you would like to pray to Him. Express your prayer as a conversation with your eyes open.

____

____

____

____

____

Fellowship with Believers

Record your progress in completing the activity you chose for this week.

Witness to the World

Record your progress in completing the activity you chose for this week.

Minister to Others

Record your progress in completing the activity you chose for this week.

DAY 3

SPEND TIME WITH THE MASTER

Refer to your journal notes for the past 10 days. Write the things God is doing with you for the benefit of others.

____

____

____

LIVE IN THE WORD

Write the reference of your selected Scripture reading for today.

____

When you read the Bible, God speaks to reveal Himself. Describe what you see God revealing about Himself in today's Scripture.

____

____

____

____

____

PRAY IN FAITH

Choose one of God's names and praise Him for being what that name represents. Write your prayer.

____

____

____

____

Fellowship with Believers

Record your progress in completing the activity you chose for this week.

Witness to the World

Record your progress in completing the activity you chose for this week.

Minister to Others

Record your progress in completing the activity you chose for this week.

DAY 4

Spend Time with the Master

On a scale of 1 to 10, with 10 being the highest, circle a number to indicate the importance of your quiet time.

1 2 3 4 5 6 7 8 9 10

Live in the Word

Write the reference of your selected Scripture reading for today.

When you read your Bible, God reveals His purposes. Explain how God's purposes are revealed in today's passage.

Pray in Faith

List the subjects of your prayers as you pray. Write a summary of each prayer subject.

Fellowship with Believers

Record your progress in completing the activity you chose for this week.

Witness to the World

Record your progress in completing the activity you chose for this week.

Minister to Others

Record your progress in completing the activity you chose for this week.

DAY 5

SPEND TIME WITH THE MASTER

As the number of names on your daily prayer list (p. 178) increases, you may not be able to pray for each request every day. Identify requests that could be put on a weekly or monthly prayer list (p. 179). Plan to pray through these lists during your extended time with God during or after week 13 (see pp. 153–54).

LIVE IN THE WORD

Write the reference of your selected Scripture reading for today.

____

God reveals His ways to show us how to live. Describe how God's ways are revealed in today's Scripture.

____

____

____

____

____

PRAY IN FAITH

God forgave Simon Peter's mistakes many times. God will forgive anyone who asks for forgiveness. Confess the shortcomings in your life that need God's merciful forgiveness. Write your prayer here.

____

____

____

____

____

Fellowship with Believers

Record your progress in completing the activity you chose for this week.

Witness to the World

Record your progress in completing the activity you chose for this week.

Minister to Others

Record your progress in completing the activity you chose for this week.

WEEK 11

WITNESS TO THE WORLD

J. DAVID CARTER

The *goal* of a Christian is to replace his or her identity with the identity of Christ. Said another way, the goal is for other persons to see the likeness of Christ in the Christian. To reach this goal, a believer must practice self-denial, bear responsibility, and follow Jesus. Jesus said, " 'If anyone would come after me, he must deny himself and take up his cross daily and follow me' " (Luke 9:23).

We reach this goal when we properly represent Christ. A Christian does not act in his or her own authority. We witness by Jesus' authority. The word *authority* means *ability, privilege, competency, and freedom.* Jesus said, " 'All authority in heaven and on earth has been given to me' " (Matt. 28:18). Authority rests in Jesus; no one else has the right to give the instructions He gives in the verses that follow. The Christian has been given an assignment to represent the One with all authority. Therefore, the Christian has all the authority needed, with the liberty and right to witness in all the world. There is no place where the witness does not have delegated authority to represent Christ.

The *task* of a Christian is to make disciples. Jesus commanded, " 'Go and make disciples of all nations, baptizing them in the name of the Father and of the Son and of the Holy Spirit' " (Matt. 28:19). The word *go* is best translated *as you go.* A Christian is instructed to give witness in his or her everyday patterns of life. As we go to work, to the grocery store, to ball games, to school, or to a business meeting, we are to represent Christ to others.

The discipline of witnessing to the world goes beyond living a good life to reaching others who will become witnesses for Christ. This is the principle of multiplication. A Christian must ask, *Am I influencing and leading others to Christ and equipping them to do the same?* This leads us to the role of a witnessing Christian.

The *role* of a Christian is to be a discipler. Jesus continued: " 'Teaching them to obey everything I have commanded you. And surely I am with you always, to the very end of the age' " (Matt. 28:20). The witness is assigned the responsibility to teach other persons to obey and do all of the things Christ commands. The primary way we do this is by doing what we instruct others to do. That is the role of the witnessing Christian.

Jesus said, " 'You will receive power when the Holy Spirit comes on you; and you will be my witnesses in Jerusalem, and in all Judea and Samaria, and to the ends of the earth' " (Acts 1:8). At our spiritual birth Christ's Spirit came to live in us. When we live in His Spirit, we experience His power. The word for *witness* in this verse is the word for *martyr*—a person who pays the price. A Christian witness volunteers to sacrifice; it is not forced but a desired choice. Jesus said: " 'Anyone who does not carry his cross and follow me cannot be my disciple. Suppose one of you wants to build a tower. Will he not first sit down and estimate the cost to see if he has enough money to complete it?' " (Luke 14:27-28). Practicing a discipline involves considering the cost of the commitment and making a decision to act on it. This is true when it comes to Christian witnessing.

The witness is assigned the responsibility of witnessing to all the world. Individually, we cannot do that, but by making disciples, we can expand our influence.

This Week's Suggested Scripture Readings

The following Scriptures support the discipline of witnessing to the world. Choose from these Scriptures to complete your "Live in the Word" assignment each day this week or substitute other Scriptures you have selected.

Day 1—Psalm 96:3; Mark 13:10-11; Acts 18:9-10; Revelation 15:4
Day 2—Isaiah 43:10-12; Luke 24:47-48; John 3:3; Acts 22:14-15
Day 3—Isaiah 49:6; Acts 26:16-18; Romans 3:23-24; 1 Corinthians 2:13
Day 4—Isaiah 51:16; John 9:1-15; Romans 6:23; Romans 10:14-15
Day 5—Matthew 16:15; John 15:27; Romans 14:11; Revelation 22:17

This Week's Suggested Memory Verses

Memorize one of the following verses this week or another verse you have selected.

- Psalm 96:3
- Romans 6:23
- Romans 10:14
- 1 Corinthians 2:13

DAY 1

Spend Time with the Master

God alerts a person's spirit when He is about to say or do something special. Be attentive to God's putting you on alert. If you are listening, you will know that it is God. List ways you will know that God is speaking.

____

____

____

Live in the Word

Write the reference of your selected Scripture reading for today.

____

It is not as important how God speaks as it is that He speaks. God always speaks through the Bible. What He says can be a general message or specifically directed. Record the general message of today's Scripture.

____

____

____

____

Pray in Faith

When God speaks, He expects a response of agreement. In prayer we tell God that we agree with Him. Record areas of your life in which you know that God is calling for agreement.

____

____

____

____

Fellowship with Believers

Choose an activity from the list on pages 165–68 to complete this week. Begin writing plans for completing it.

Witness to the World

Choose an activity from the list on pages 169–72 to complete this week. Begin writing plans for completing it.

Minister to Others

Choose an activity from the list on pages 173–76 to complete this week. Begin writing plans for completing it.

DAY 2

SPEND TIME WITH THE MASTER

Listening to God is a continuous process that is not confined to your quiet time. Be on call for God. Recall a method God has used to get your attention and write a lesson you learned.

LIVE IN THE WORD

Write the reference of your selected Scripture reading for today.

Yesterday you recorded the general message of a Scripture. Today record the message you feel is specifically for you.

PRAY IN FAITH

As you meditate on that personal message from Scripture, make brief notes on your thoughts. Write a prayer response.

Fellowship with Believers

Record your progress in completing the activity you chose for this week.

Witness to the World

Record your progress in completing the activity you chose for this week.

Minister to Others

Record your progress in completing the activity you chose for this week.

DAY 3

Spend Time with the Master

God does not have to get our attention if we are listening. Write ways you listen to God.

____

____

____

Live in the Word

Write the reference of your selected Scripture reading for today.

____

God's Word is sometimes compared to food (see 1 Pet. 2:2-3). What nourishment do you need from God's Word today?

____

____

____

Pray in Faith

Name two areas of your life in which you need strength. Write and pray something like this: Lord, You are my nourishment. I need You to strengthen me where otherwise I would be weak.

____

____

____

____

____

____

Fellowship with Believers

Record your progress in completing the activity you chose for this week.

Witness to the World

Record your progress in completing the activity you chose for this week.

Minister to Others

Record your progress in completing the activity you chose for this week.

DAY 4

Spend Time with the Master

Listening is done with your spirit as well as with your senses. Describe ways you know that God is speaking to your spirit.

Live in the Word

Write the reference of your selected Scripture reading for today.

As you read today's Scripture, assume the physical position you consider most reverent. Describe how you feel as you read God's Word in that position.

Pray in Faith

Name one area of your life that is usually closed to God. Write and pray a prayer something like this: Redeemer, speak to the area of my life that is usually closed to You.

Fellowship with Believers

Record your progress in completing the activity you chose for this week.

Witness to the World

Record your progress in completing the activity you chose for this week.

Minister to Others

Record your progress in completing the activity you chose for this week.

DAY 5

Spend Time with the Master

God wants us to experience His kingdom. Kingdom living lifts you above human limitations. To walk in the Spirit is to live in the kingdom. Name actions you can take to live in the kingdom.

____

____

____

Live in the Word

Write the reference of your selected Scripture reading for today.

____

God loves you. Record something from your Scripture passage that assures you of that.

____

____

____

____

Pray in Faith

Sit quietly and listen to God tell you how much He loves you. Describe the way God regards you as His child.

____

____

____

____

____

Fellowship with Believers

Record your progress in completing the activity you chose for this week.

Witness to the World

Record your progress in completing the activity you chose for this week.

Minister to Others

Record your progress in completing the activity you chose for this week.

WEEK 12

Minister to Others

AVERY T. WILLIS, JR.

Jesus called us to follow Him and to be involved in ministry with Him: "He appointed twelve—designating them apostles—that they might be with him and that he might send them out to preach and to have authority to drive out demons" (Mark 3:14-15). How long is the time between following and serving? For the disciples it was not long before they started, but it was at least three years before they really understood what Jesus wanted them to do. Even at the end of His earthly ministry they still wanted to be served rather than to serve. Jesus told them: " 'The kings of the Gentiles lord it over them; and those who exercise authority over them call themselves Benefactors. But you are not to be like that. Instead, the greatest among you should be like the youngest, and the one who rules like the one who serves. For who is greater, the one who is at the table or the one who serves? Is it not the one who is at the table? But I am among you as one who serves' " (Luke 22:25-27).

The disciples ignored His teaching. At the Last Supper Jesus, approaching His time to be crucified, took bold action to teach the disciples to be servants. He washed their feet.

> "Do you understand what I have done for you?" he asked them. "You call me 'Teacher' and 'Lord,' and rightly so, for that is what I am. Now that I, your Lord and Teacher, have washed your feet, you also should wash one another's feet. I have set you an example that you should do as I have done for you. I tell you the truth, no servant is greater than his master, nor is a messenger greater than the one who sent him. Now that you know these things, you will be blessed if you do them" (John 13:12-17).

We learn several lessons about ministry from Jesus. First, a servant uses the same pattern Jesus used to minister. Jesus set an example. He is our model. When we examine the account closer, the words shock us: "Jesus knew that the Father had put all things under his power, and that he had come from God and was returning to God; so he got up from the meal, took off his outer clothing, and wrapped a towel around his waist" (John 13:3-4). What a contrast! Jesus was aware of the time, His disciples, His power, and His future state; yet He dared to wash their feet. In doing so, Jesus revealed that God is a servant God; He ministers to others. Jesus humbled Himself to come to earth and serve people (see Phil. 2:5-8). How can we refuse to serve people? How can we pattern ourselves after the world's models once we have experienced His serving us? Jesus set the pattern for our service and ministry.

Second, a servant serves the kind of people Jesus served. None of us would have served such a band of 12 ordinary men for three years. In addition, Jesus ministered to the sick, the blind, the outcasts, the rich, the poor, the self-righteous, and the prostitutes. How different are you from the people you serve? Are you serving the people who really need it, or are you serving yourself and those who can help you in return?

Third, a servant serves with the Master's power and resources. Even after Jesus had given the disciples authority over evil spirits, they failed to cast the evil spirit out of a boy because they tried to do it in their power rather than spend time in prayer. Peter finally learned the lesson after Jesus' death and resurrection. He said to the crippled man: " 'Silver or gold I do not have, but what I have I give you. In the name of Jesus Christ of Nazareth, walk' " (Acts 3:6). A servant must depend on the Master for power and resources. Any servant, no matter how weak or insignificant, can serve when he or she depends on God to supply what is needed.

God is looking for servants to minister to others as He did.

This Week's Suggested Scripture Readings

The following Scriptures support the discipline of ministering to others. Choose from these Scriptures to complete your "Live in the Word" assignment each day this week or substitute other Scriptures you have selected.

Day 1—Psalm 2:11; Matthew 10:42; 1 Corinthians 3:11-14; Hebrews 13:16
Day 2—Psalm 126:5-6; Matthew 25:31-46; Galatians 6:2; James 2:14-18
Day 3—Isaiah 1:19; Luke 6:35; Ephesians 6:7-8; 1 Peter 2:12
Day 4—John 4:34; Acts 20:24; Romans 7:6; 1 Thessalonians 2:8
Day 5—John 15:13; Romans 12:1; 1 Timothy 6:18; Hebrews 13:1-3

This Week's Suggested Memory Verses

Memorize one of the following verses this week or another verse you have selected.

- Psalm 126:5
- Acts 20:24
- Romans 12:1
- Galatians 6:2

DAY 1

Spend Time with the Master
We sin when we know we should do certain things but do not do them. Name one of these things and explain why you are not doing it.

____

____

Live in the Word
Write the reference of your selected Scripture reading for today.

____

After you read today's Scripture, complete this sentence:

When God speaks to me like this, I—

____

____

____

Pray in Faith
Prayer is one way we respond when we realize that God has taken the initiative to have a relationship with us. Read your prayer notes for the past 10 days and ask God to remind you of what He has been saying. Record the main ideas below. If God has given you a special message, write it in "Spiritual Markers" on page 180.

____

____

____

____

____

Fellowship with Believers

Choose an activity from the list on pages 165–68 to complete this week. Begin writing plans for completing it.

Witness to the World

Choose an activity from the list on pages 169–72 to complete this week. Begin writing plans for completing it.

Minister to Others

Choose an activity from the list on pages 173–76 to complete this week. Begin writing plans for completing it.

DAY 2

Spend Time with the Master

Yesterday you named something you should be doing that you are not. What decisions do you need to make to begin that activity?

Live in the Word

Write the reference of your selected Scripture reading for today.

Based on your Scripture passage, describe a thought that needs to be replaced with God's Word.

Pray in Faith

To pray without ceasing means that we are on alert for a word from God. Write a prayer in which you let God know that you want to give Him your attention today.

Fellowship with Believers

Record your progress in completing the activity you chose for this week.

Witness to the World

Record your progress in completing the activity you chose for this week.

Minister to Others

Record your progress in completing the activity you chose for this week.

DAY 3

Spend Time with the Master

Meditate on the idea that Christ is always with you. What does that reality mean to you today?

Live in the Word

Write the reference of your selected Scripture reading for today.

Set a goal by praying, I want to develop the mind of Christ by renewing 10 of my memory verses. List the references of these verses.

Pray in Faith

Write a prayer in which you ask God to help you replace impure thoughts with those that are pure and holy.

Fellowship with Believers

Record your progress in completing the activity you chose for this week.

Witness to the World

Record your progress in completing the activity you chose for this week.

Minister to Others

Record your progress in completing the activity you chose for this week.

DAY 4

Spend Time with the Master

Review your plans for spending an extended time with God one day next week or after next week (see pp. 153–54). Be prepared to face opposition to scheduling that time. Describe what you can do to make that time a priority.

Live in the Word

Write the reference of your selected Scripture reading for today.

Purity is God's standard for Christian living. The opposite of purity is impurity. The perversion of purity is being puritanical. Describe how God has used or is using His Word to convict you of impure or puritanical behavior.

Pray in Faith

Ask God to give you strength to win spiritual battles as you are tested and tried. Write your prayer here.

Fellowship with Believers

Record your progress in completing the activity you chose for this week.

Witness to the World

Record your progress in completing the activity you chose for this week.

Minister to Others

Record your progress in completing the activity you chose for this week.

DAY 5

Spend Time with the Master
Identify something you need to do to strengthen your quiet time.

Live in the Word
Write the reference of your selected Scripture reading for today.

"Faith cometh by hearing and hearing by the word of God" (Rom. 10:17, KJV). Identify an area of your life in which your faith is being tested.

Pray in Faith
Choose one of the Ten Commandments you have the most difficulty obeying. Write it below. Ask God to help you love that commandment.

Fellowship with Believers

Record your progress in completing the activity you chose for this week.

Witness to the World

Record your progress in completing the activity you chose for this week.

Minister to Others

Record your progress in completing the activity you chose for this week.

WEEK 13

SPEND AN EXTENDED TIME WITH GOD

†

AVERY T. WILLIS, JR.

You have reached the final week of *Day by Day in God's Kingdom.* As you approach the end of this 13-week journey, you will want to schedule a three-hour period during or after this week for an extended time with God. You will use this time to—

- have extended, uninterrupted fellowship with God;
- evaluate what God has been doing and saying in your life during the past 13 weeks;
- solidify Christ's lordship in all aspects of your life;
- receive guidance for future spiritual growth and ministry;
- concentrate prayer on your major concerns;
- intercede for others.

Here are ways to spend your extended time with God.

- Review your journal to detect any patterns in what God has said to you and/or in what you have said to Him. Note the answers to your prayers, evidences of spiritual growth, helpful insights, and commitments or concerns you need to pray about.
- Read your Bible. Listen to God speak to you. Meditate on your Scripture-memory verses.
- Use your prayer lists (pp. 178–79) to pray for your needs and others' needs.
- Write your goals for spiritual growth and ministry. Pray about actions you need to take.
- Use different types of prayer, such as confession, thanksgiving, and praise.
- Listen to God at least as much as you talk to Him.

What if you keep thinking of other things as you try to pray?

- Pray for whatever occurs to you. Perhaps God placed that thought in your mind so that you will deal with a certain issue.
- Write down things to do later so that you can forget them now.
- List things that continually come to mind. Ask God why. You are not preparing a speech to give to God. You are communicating with Him mind to mind, heart to heart, and spirit to Spirit. You are dialoguing with Him even as you think.

Here are some ideas for making meaningful your extended time with God.

- Keep notes on what you do. Write down the time you begin and complete each activity.

- Consult your notes in preparation for your next extended time with God to ensure balance in your prayers. For example, if you spent most of this time praying about your needs, next time pray more for the needs of others.

Try to have an extended time with God once a month. Also plan a time with Him when—

- you want to glorify God and express your love to Him;
- you need fellowship with the Master;
- you need guidance or strength;
- you face a critical or new phase of ministry;
- you need spiritual awakening;
- others need your prayers;
- laborers are needed for the harvest.[1]

This Week's Suggested Scripture Readings

The following Scriptures emphasize the need to grow in Christ. Choose from these Scriptures to complete your "Live in the Word" assignment each day this week or substitute other Scriptures you have selected.

Day 1—Deuteronomy 30:19-20; Romans 6:12-13; 2 Corinthians 7:1; Colossians 2:6-7; Hebrews 6:1

Day 2—Psalm 15; Romans 12:2-3; Galatians 5:22-25; Hebrews 12:1-2; James 1:4

Day 3—Psalm 55:22; 1 Corinthians 1:8-9; Ephesians 4:11-15; Philippians 3:13-14; 1 Peter 2:1-3

Day 4—Psalm 92:12-15; 1 Corinthians 6:19-20; Ephesians 3:16-19; Ephesians 6:10-18; 2 Peter 3:18

Day 5—Psalm 147:11; Ephesians 4:1; 2 Corinthians 5:9-10; Philippians 1:6; Jude 24-25

This Week's Suggested Memory Verses

Memorize one of the following verses this week or another verse you have selected.

- Psalm 55:22
- Romans 12:2-3
- Galatians 5:22-23
- Philippians 3:13-14

DAY 1

Spend Time with the Master

Begin your quiet time by asking God to show you anything in your life that should not be present. Write down anything He reveals.

Live in the Word

Write the reference of your selected Scripture reading for today.

The Bible calls Jesus the life (see John 14:6). Write two treasured values of having Him as your life.

Pray in Faith

Write general plans for an extended time with God during or after this week. Schedule a time to update your prayer lists (pp. 178–79) in preparation for your extended time with God.

Fellowship with Believers

Choose an activity from the list on pages 165–68 to complete this week. Begin writing plans for completing it.

Witness to the World

Choose an activity from the list on pages 169–72 to complete this week. Begin writing plans for completing it.

Minister to Others

Choose an activity from the list on pages 173–76 to complete this week. Begin writing plans for completing it.

DAY 2

Spend Time with the Master
Review your journal notes for the past 12 weeks to see how many goals you have reached. List one or more of those goals and write a statement after each one that expresses your feelings.

____

____

____

____

____

____

Live in the Word
Write the reference of your selected Scripture reading for today.

____

Review your journal notes for week 1. Identify one area in your Bible reading in which you have grown. Describe your feelings about experiencing measurable growth.

____

____

____

____

Pray in Faith
Write the name of someone you will contact today to pray for you. Do this regardless of whether you have a great need.

____

Fellowship with Believers

Record your progress in completing the activity you chose for this week.

Witness to the World

Record your progress in completing the activity you chose for this week.

Minister to Others

Record your progress in completing the activity you chose for this week.

DAY 3

Spend Time with the Master
Complete the following sentence.

My daily quiet time has impressed on me the fact that God—

____

____

____

____

Live in the Word
Write the reference of your selected Scripture reading for today.

____

Review your life verse. Identify two or three times when God has used it to give you the assurance of His presence in your life.

____

____

____

____

Pray in Faith
Schedule a time for tomorrow when you can have a 10- to 15-minute prayer walk. Make notes below about subjects you would like to pray about as you walk.

____

____

____

Fellowship with Believers

Record your progress in completing the activity you chose for this week.

Witness to the World

Record your progress in completing the activity you chose for this week.

Minister to Others

Record your progress in completing the activity you chose for this week.

DAY 4

Spend Time with the Master
Write a schedule for your extended time with God, which you will have this week or next week. A plan is suggested on pages 153–54. Feel free to adjust the activities.

Live in the Word
Write the reference of your selected Scripture reading for today.

Identify a verse from today's reading that seems to have a message for you. Meditate on it and write its meaning for you.

Pray in Faith
Choose a main thought from the Scripture you are memorizing this week and write it in the form of a prayer.

Fellowship with Believers

Record your progress in completing the activity you chose for this week.

____

____

____

____

____

Witness to the World

Record your progress in completing the activity you chose for this week.

____

____

____

____

____

Minister to Others

Record your progress in completing the activity you chose for this week.

____

____

____

____

____

DAY 5

Spend Time with the Master

Three months ago you began using this journal. Summarize differences you have noticed in your quiet time.

Live in the Word

Write the reference of your selected Scripture reading for today.

Review your journal notes and identify two or three verses that have meant the most to you in the past three months. Briefly state why.

Pray in Faith

Review your prayer lists (pp. 178–79) and summarize the prayers that have been answered.

Fellowship with Believers

Record your progress in completing the activity you chose for this week.

____

____

____

____

____

Witness to the World

Record your progress in completing the activity you chose for this week.

____

____

____

____

____

Minister to Others

Record your progress in completing the activity you chose for this week.

____

____

____

____

____

[1]Adapted from Avery T. Willis, Jr., *MasterLife 3: The Disciple's Victory* (Nashville: LifeWay Press, 1996), 119, 123–24.

Fellowship with Believers

J. DAVID CARTER

Following are suggestions for practicing the discipline of fellowshipping with believers. Choose a different activity to complete each week. Some activities require more time and commitment than others. Make realistic choices that reflect your commitment to grow in this area of your Christian life. After choosing an activity for the week on day 1, use the next four days' material in your journal to record your plans for and progress in completing that activity.

- Encourage several believers.
- Choose a family member and spend time in conversation with him or her.
- Express gratitude to your pastor or another church-staff member for the role he or she plays in your life.
- Identify a fellow church member with whom you want to develop a stronger relationship and take the person to lunch at your expense.
- Visit a fellow church member who recently lost a loved one to death.
- Spend a half day as a volunteer meeting a church need.
- Tell the strongest Christian you know what his or her strength means to you.
- Help a new Christian begin a plan of discipleship using *Survival Kit.*[1] Work through the first day's lesson with the person and plan to talk each week about the person's work on daily lessons.
- Visit someone who seems to be struggling to attend church regularly. Ask him or her what you can do to help. Invite someone else to help you.
- Be alert to a statement that expresses someone's decision to grow stronger as a Christian, such as "My faith needs to be stronger." Offer to tell about a struggle in your life that strengthened your faith. Offer your support and encouragement.
- Ask God to lead you in ministering to someone who is no longer active in your church. Visit and pray with the person.
- Write what today's Scripture passage suggests about your role in nurturing the spiritual growth of a friend.
- Rebuild a relationship with someone by ministering to him or her.
- Nurture a mature Christian through a ministry of encouragement.
- Explain today's Scripture passage to another believer.
- Be alert to a time when God intervenes in your life and asks you to join Him in something He is doing in the life of a friend or associate. Be ready to respond as He directs.
- Send a card encouraging another believer who has a bad attitude.

- Invite a friend or a couple to have coffee or soft drink with you after an evening worship service.
- Visit someone who has a persistent prayer need and pray with the person.
- Write a letter to someone from your past who made a valuable contribution to your Christian development. Describe your present walk with the Lord and express gratitude for the value of his or her investment in your life.
- When someone stays on your mind, God may be calling you to minister to that person. Contact the person and ask how things are going. Be alert to a ministry opportunity.
- Name several persons who are trying to grow in Christ but need help. Consider leading a *MasterLife*[2] group for them.
- Invite someone you are discipling to go with you on church visitation.
- Minister to a homebound person. Invite someone you are discipling to join you on this visit. Be alert to the ministry needs of the homebound person and the person who joins you.
- Write letters or cards to persons who do not regularly attend church.
- Bow on your knees and think of someone to whom you need to submit. Jesus washed His apostles' feet. How would you feel if the person to whom you needed to submit washed your feet?
- Give a testimony about the benefits of your quiet time to another believer who is not having one.
- Look for an opportunity to quote a verse you have memorized during a conversation with another believer this week.
- If you do not already have one, choose at least one person with whom you can be an accountability partner.
- Identify behaviors or characteristics you may need to change to improve your ability to relate to other persons. Beside these characteristics write statements of steps you will take to change them.
- You are an example to others. Identify elements in your life that, if they were seen, would discourage someone.
- Teach a lesson you have learned from Scripture to another believer.
- The difference between teaching and instruction is the difference between knowing and doing. What do you know that you are not doing? Your witness to others is strengthened when you do what you say you believe.
- Spiritual needs are not easily recognized. Depend on God's using you to help others even when you do not see a spiritual need. Describe what God can do to help you surrender to His use.
- Pray for someone you plan to ask to join you for a visit to another believer who has a problem.
- List steps you can take to strengthen the organization of your church that seems the weakest.
- Describe the steps for reaching the next level of Christlike growth.

- Write a promise Christ made as He gave the Great Commission (see Matt. 28:19-20).
- Spiritual warfare is necessary to spiritual victory. Who do you know who needs your help in spiritual warfare?
- Has God led you into every church job you now have? List the tasks you are certain God wants you to do.
- Write the name of someone who could be your mentor. Write the particular trait in the person's life that you want to develop in your life.
- Name someone who has regularly turned to you for help. Consider becoming a mentor to that person.
- Identify what you can do to stimulate persons to service and ministry.
- Be attentive to a believer who is hurting and discover ways to meet the person's needs.
- If you know someone who is discouraged about his or her Christian growth, write the person a note or a card of encouragement.
- Ask a fellow Christian to give his or her personal Christian testimony as you listen and affirm; then give yours.
- Each disciple develops as a Christian at a different pace. Identify someone who has been steady and consistent in spiritual growth. What does your relationship with that person mean to you?
- Identify a personal friend. Name other persons involved in this friend's discipleship.
- What Christian resource, such as the Bible, prayer, fellowship with other believers, or witnessing, is most valuable to help you develop your spiritual nature and reject your sinful nature? Why?
- Write a short report about one person you are discipling and what you are doing to help.
- Write a brief definition of *responsibility* as it relates to fellowshipping with believers. Compare your definition with the responsibility Jesus assumed when He died on the cross.
- Write a goal for developing a quality or habit related to the discipline of fellowshipping with believers.
- Describe what you will do to improve your relationship with a family member or a friend.
- List the strong points in your relationships with other believers. As you list them, give Scripture verses that can strengthen you in these areas.
- "Carry each other's burdens, and in this way you will fulfill the law of Christ" (Gal. 6:2). Who is carrying a burden you can bear? Name the burden and describe how you will begin to carry it for your friend.
- Jesus exhibited five fundamental qualities as He developed Christlikeness in His disciples. On the following page rate your strength in each quality by circling one of the numbers on a scale of 1 to 5, with 1 being weakest and 5 being most like Jesus.

Love	1	2	3	4	5
Respect	1	2	3	4	5
Faith/expectation	1	2	3	4	5
Trust/delegation	1	2	3	4	5
Honesty	1	2	3	4	5

- List the names of persons you have nurtured in their faith during the past three months.
- Name the person most involved in nurturing your spiritual growth. What are you most thankful for in that person?

---

[1]*Survival Kit* is a six-week, interactive workbook that helps establish new believers in their Christian lives. Order item 0-8054-9770-6 from the Customer Service Center; 127 Ninth Avenue, North; Nashville, TN 37234; 1-800-458-2772; or purchase at a Baptist Book Store or a Lifeway Christian Store.

[2]*MasterLife* is an in-depth discipleship process that involves the study of interactive workbooks and attendance at group sessions. For information about *MasterLife* write to Adult Discipleship and Family Department, MSN 151; 127 Ninth Avenue, North; Nashville, TN 37234-0151.

Witness to the World

J. DAVID CARTER

Following are suggestions for practicing the discipline of witnessing to the world. Choose a different activity to complete each week. Some activities require more time and commitment than others. Make realistic choices that reflect your commitment to grow in this area of your Christian life. After choosing an activity for the week on day 1, use the next four days' material in your journal to record your plans for and progress in completing that activity.

- Valid witnessing begins with placing high value on the persons you want to reach. Name ways you will place value on persons with whom you want to earn the right to present the gospel.
- The life circle shown below represents your relationships. Write on your life circle the names of the five persons who are closest to you.

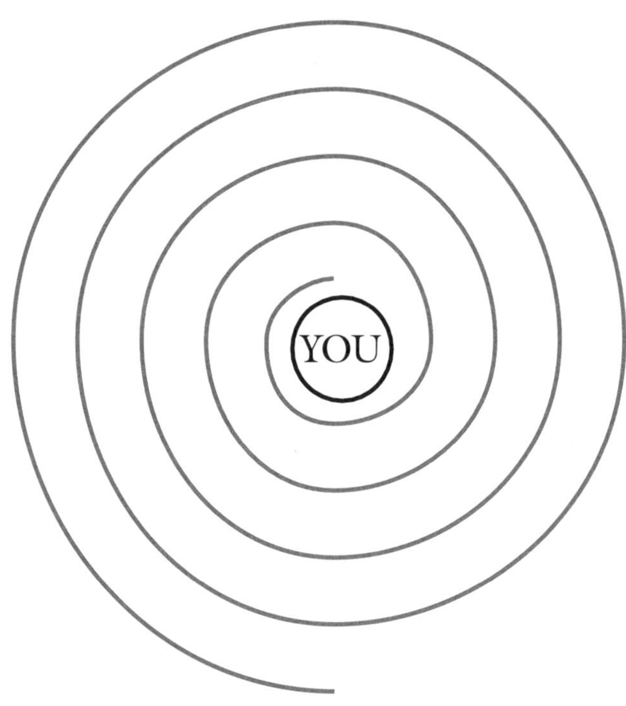

Life Circle

- Begin a list of unchurched and unsaved persons in your life circle (p. 169). Add their names to one of your prayer lists (pp. 178–79).
- When witnessing, spend more time listening than talking. Purposely make yourself available to listen to a couple of associates as they talk about what is happening in their lives.
- Invite an unsaved friend to join you in a hobby or another activity.
- Add the name of an unsaved friend to one of your prayer lists (pp. 178–79). Invite this person to attend church. Give a testimony of your personal faith in Christ.
- Enlist someone to role-play a witnessing encounter with you. Practice presenting the gospel to this person, who should assume the role of a seeker who wants to talk about Christ but is not ready to make a commitment.
- Practice giving your personal Christian testimony without using church or theological words.
- List the names of non-Christian friends with whom you have long-term relationships. Recall times when you were with the friends during difficult times. How did you use those times as open doors to present the gospel?
- Many Christians are participating in overseas evangelism projects. Are you willing to go? Consider volunteering.
- Obtain the names of church prospects and make appointments to visit them. Make two visits during one evening.
- Write ways your church can expand its efforts to reach the lost.
- Volunteer to give your personal Christian testimony during a worship service.
- Be attentive to a teenager who is in trouble with the law. Visit the family's home to have prayer.
- How many persons in your life circle (p. 169) have unsaved family members? Write ways you can help reach these persons.
- Financial gifts enable others to do full-time missionary work. Begin or expand your giving plan for missions. Write an amount you would like to give if you had the money. Then write an amount you are able to give. One is based on God's supplying it, and the other is based on what God has already supplied.
- Write a note to your pastor that affirms the church's evangelistic efforts.
- Look for an opportunity to interview someone who recently made a profession of faith in your church. Ask: What was the strongest motivation for your becoming a Christian? Do you know someone who needs this same experience? Ask if the person would accompany you to visit that prospect.
- Add the names of lost persons to your life circle (p. 169). Beside each name write strategies you will use to cultivate a relationship with the person and to give a witness.
- Write the name of a child or a teenage family member who has not

received Christ. Look for an opportunity to express your concern for this person's salvation.

- The desire to be involved in bringing persons to faith in Christ should be a strong force in our lives. On a scale of 1 to 10, with 10 being the highest, write the number that represents how strong this desire is in your life. Then answer the question, Why? over the next four days.
- Make an appointment to visit a lost person. Be prepared to listen more than talk.
- During a weekend, talk with your immediate family about the importance of your faith in Christ. Give testimonies to children and adults alike.
- Write the name of someone who seems to resist talking about religion. Begin cultivating a relationship by talking about the person's choice of subjects. Add this person's name to one of your prayer lists (pp. 178–79).
- List your neighbors' names—children and adults. If you do not know all of the names, take measures to learn them. Make a special effort to call each neighbor by name.
- Talk to your neighbors about having a neighborhood cookout. Plan how you can share your faith and the reasons you attend church.
- Ask unchurched neighbors if you may invite their children to attend church with you or your children.
- Invite lost neighbors to join you in attending a special event at church, such as a singing group or a special speaker.
- Find a way to serve your neighbor. For example, bake a cake and give half to the neighbor on each side of you.
- You do not have to prepare a major presentation to introduce the gospel. Look for little things you can say or do that will call attention to the gospel.
- Ask God to help you begin a conversation with a business associate by asking, "What do you think our world will be like if crime continues to increase?" Allow several minutes of discussion; then say, "I know what the world needs, but it is very difficult to get some people to believe it."
- Choose a gospel tract to leave with clerks, servers, and other persons you meet during the week. Begin a practice of using tracts with positive messages.
- Plan to arrive early at church. Stand at the edge of the parking lot to look for persons who are new to your church. As they park their cars, welcome them and offer to help them find their destinations.
- Choose someone who has been attending your church but has not joined. Ask him or her to join you for lunch at your home or at a restaurant.
- Identify someone to join you for special seasonal church services.
- If a special women's or men's meeting is scheduled at your church, whom would you like to invite who is not yet a church member?

- Visit the homes of from two to four prospects. Give your personal Christian testimony and ask if they have had experiences like yours. If not, offer to help them make that decision.
- Whom do you know who seems to need the Lord the most? Write a strategy you will implement to present the gospel.
- Write the name of an older relative who has not received Christ. Ask God to give you the wisdom to write a letter expressing your concern for his or her salvation.
- Look for a time during a business meal with an unchurched associate to ask permission to talk about your faith in Christ. After receiving permission, explain the steps a person takes to be assured of going to heaven.
- Volunteer to give your testimony in a youth Sunday School class and to tell the students how to become Christians.
- If you have children, plan an uninterrupted time to present the gospel to each.
- Make a telephone call to a long-distance friend and give your Christian testimony.
- Review your life circle (p. 169). Place checks beside the names of those who have come to Christ.
- Refer to your prayer lists (pp. 178–79) and underline the names of persons you have most recently added who need salvation. Describe what you are doing to win one of these persons.
- Witnessing is not optional. What actions will you take to make your witnessing efforts more effective in leading persons to faith in Christ?

Minister to Others

J. David Carter

Following are suggestions for practicing the discipline of ministering to others. Choose a different activity to complete each week. Some activities require more time and commitment than others. Make realistic choices that reflect your commitment to grow in this area of your Christian life. After choosing an activitv for the week on day 1, use the next four days' material in your journal to record your plans for and progress in completing that activity.

- Each day this week name a ministry Jesus did and describe how you can be like Jesus in performing that ministry.
- Jesus supernaturally fed five thousand people with five loaves of bread and two fish (see Matt. 14:13-21). How can you feed the hungry? Give money or do something else to feed others, such as serving meals in a rescue center for a week.
- Jesus touched the untouchable leper (see Matt. 8:1-3). Are there untouchables in your life? What can you do to figuratively touch an untouchable in Christ's love?
- Recall the parable of the Good Samaritan (see Luke 10:25-37). What one lesson can you apply in ministering to others?
- Describe a ministry your church has to children. State the degree of involvement to which you are ready to commit.
- Name something you can offer as a ministry of your church and begin counting your costs.
- People have physical, emotional, social, spiritual, and financial needs. Write the name of someone you can minister to and name the need.
- List five ministries of your church that reach persons who are not church members.
- God shows us a need and invites us to join Him in meeting that need. Name an area of ministry in which God could be asking you to join Him.
- Recall someone who accepted Christ because your church ministered to him or her. Name a lost person to whom you can minister.
- Describe a new ministry your church could provide. What has to be done to begin this ministry? What are you willing to do?
- List three personal strengths that could be used in ministry.
- List up to four persons in your church who have expressed interest in the same type ministry that interests you. Name this ministry and ask God to show you your role.
- Name two or three persons who could benefit from your ministry of prayer. Send them notes or call to tell them that you are praying for them. Schedule a time to pray with them.

- Jesus wants us to model our ministries after Him. Name one situation in which Jesus ministered as a teacher. Does God want you to have a ministry as a teacher? What subject would be most interesting for you to teach?
- Some parents need to break cycles of behavior that damage their children with patterns they learned from their parents. Name one or more of those patterns and describe what your church can do to help parents break the cycle of hurtful family experiences.
- The nuclear family is a minority in our society. Name the different family structures in your church. Does your church's commitment to reach nuclear families preclude a ministry to nontraditional families, such as single-parent families? What does your church need to do to expand ministries to nontraditional families?
- List two churchwide outreach projects that need your involvement.
- Name a person who ministers effectively to persons outside the church. Interview him or her and ask, "What can I do to strengthen my prayer ministry?" Write down the answers. Of these responses which are you ready to do? Which will require more growth?
- An offer to pray opens the door to further ministry. A very effective ministry is listening. Ask someone, "Is anything happening in your life that you would like me to pray about?" Then listen without reply.
- Identify from three to five persons who have recently experienced grief. Send them cards of encouragement.
- Some of the persons who need ministry the most are those whose lives seem to be going well. Write the names of two of these persons. Make yourself available by asking God to put you in a situation in which you can minister.
- Be sensitive to prayer requests made during church prayer times. Approach one of the persons who requested prayer and offer your prayer support.
- Name two new ministries you have identified in the past few weeks as you practiced the discipline of ministering to others.
- In the next two minutes list ministries you know that other churches are doing but your church is not. Circle the ministry that you consider to be beyond anything your church is ready to do. List one statement each day for a week that summarizes what needs to be done to implement that ministry.
- What is the easiest ministry you could help your church start? Who is the best person to be responsible for it? Approach that person and share your impressions.
- Although all churches should minister, not every church is meant to do the same ministries as other churches. This is also true for individuals. Name ministries unique to you and your church.
- Set a goal to help your church start a new ministry. Write that goal. Include it on one of your prayer lists (pp. 178–79).

- Recall a person in the Bible whom Jesus healed. Describe the attitude Jesus expressed. Ask yourself whether you have that attitude.
- Recall a time when Jesus healed someone. The healing Jesus gave was loving and accepting. List one action you can take each day for the next four days to be more loving and accepting.
- Describe an obstacle you have experienced in starting a new ministry. Record a benefit of the ministry each day for the next four days.
- Write a potential new ministry and the persons' names who would receive the ministry. As you perform the ministry, record each day for the next four days the effect it has on your life.
- Identify a need for financial assistance by listing possible names or situations and plan to give an amount of money to help meet this need. Ask God to help you identify who is to receive the money. Deliver the money this week or have it delivered anonymously. Tell the person that you wrote your plans in your daily journal and that God helped you know whom to give the money to. Record in your journal over the next four days what it cost you to give the money. Describe the costs in other than financial terms.
- If you regularly gave money to needy persons, what do you think your long-term attitudes and lifestyle would be?
- Describe a long-term ministry in which you feel that God can use you. Over the next four days record 3-, 6-, 9-, and 12-month goals for the ministry.
- As long-term ministries grow, you will also grow. Jesus wants us to count the costs. What are some costs of long-term ministries?
- Long-term ministries usually involve more persons than the ones starting them. What are the long-term ministries in your church? Describe the characteristics of the persons who started one of them.
- Ordinary persons do extraordinary ministry when God is in it. Describe the requirements for your experiencing God's long-term, supernatural activity.
- What obstacles do you have to overcome in your life to establish a stable, long-term ministry? List them.
- If you are willing to begin a new ministry but know that you are doing all God wants you to do, ask God to show you someone you could tell about your dreams for a new ministry.
- What adjustments do you need to make to join God on mission?
- What ministry is God inviting you or your church to do? What can you do to make this happen?
- What did you learn from today's Scripture that applies to the ministry most important to you? Record a lesson from your Scripture each day for the next four days.
- During your prayer times this week record what God says that you need in your ministry.
- Record the greatest hurdle to your church's expanding its areas of

ministry. How can that hurdle be overcome? What can you do to help overcome it?
- What experiences in your daily life could you use to benefit your ministry to others?
- Ministries require financial support. Record forms of individual and corporate giving to support ministry.
- What is your family's greatest need in practicing the ministry of prayer and intercession? What are you doing to meet that need?
- Who in your family most needs a ministry of nurture?
- Does your life give evidence, by the way you minister to the hurting, that you spend time with the Master? How?
- Schedule a time when your immediate family can gather for a time of fellowship and prayer.
- Describe the ministry that costs you the most but gives you the greatest blessing.
- Review ministries you have identified that you or your church could perform. Choose one and describe its status now, compared to three months ago.
- Describe how your view of ministry has expanded over the past three months.

How to Maintain Prayer Lists

Organizing your thoughts in prayer is one way to show your reverence for God (see Eccl. 5:2). Prayer lists help you cover all of the areas for which you need to pray. Ongoing prayer lists are provided on the following pages for recording daily, weekly, and monthly prayer concerns.

- *Daily* (p. 178). Keep a list of persons and subjects you pray for daily. Include members of your family, your pastor, close friends, those in authority over you, and temporary concerns.
- *Weekly* (p. 179). For each day of the week make a separate list of concerns you pray for on the same day each week. These weekly lists should include friends, church concerns, governments, elected officials, and missionaries.
- *Monthly* (p. 179). For each day of the month make a list that includes items of importance or concern but somewhat removed from your immediate situation.

You may move your requests from one list to another as you wish, and you may photocopy the lists as needed. Each time you add a request, you assume additional responsibility to pray. If maintaining prayer lists is new to you, begin where you are and develop your lists as your prayer ministry develops.

Identifying Spiritual Markers

When God gets ready for you to take the next step or direction in His activity, it will always be in sequence with what He has already been doing in your life."[1] God loves us and wants to involve us in His supernatural activity. Sometimes He interrupts our regular routine and uses us in a special way. Use the chart on page 180 to keep records of those instances. You may photocopy the chart as needed. God's interruption may come while hearing a sermon, while reading your Bible, or while talking to a friend. It may come through a crisis when He reveals characteristics of His nature to help you maintain stability in a storm of life. It may come with a sense of peace when you normally respond with stress and anxiety. A spiritual marker identifies a time of transition, decision, or direction when you clearly know that God has provided guidance.[2]

---

[1]Henry T. Blackaby and Claude V. King, *Experiencing God: Knowing and Doing the Will of God* (Nashville: LifeWay Press, 1990), 101.
[2]Ibid., 103.

Daily Prayer List

Date	Person	Need	Bible Promise	Answer

Weekly Prayer List

Date	Person	Need	Bible Promise	Answer

Monthly Prayer List

Date	Person	Need	Bible Promise	Answer

Spiritual Markers

Date	Marker	Bible Reference	Decision Made